DATE DUE			

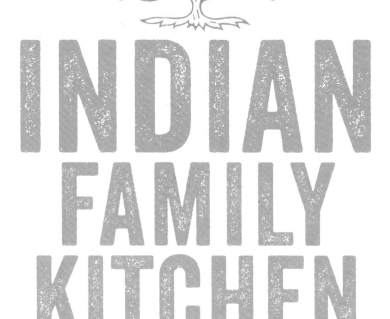

THE INDIAN FAMILY KITCHEN

CLASSIC DISHES FOR A NEW GENERATION

Anjali Pathak

CLARKSON POTTER/PUBLISHERS
NEW YORK

To my mother,
the best cook I will ever know.

Contents

Introduction

I've been fond of food from an early age, but mostly Indian food, and I've always loved cooking. My earliest memory of being in the kitchen was when my grandmother bought me a small rolling pin and board to help her make the rotis for the family dinner. She pronounced, "If you can make them round, you will find a good husband," and as a little girl I thought this was rather strange. But day after day I would sit with my board and pin, concentrating on trying to get my rotis perfectly round. This was our time together, and I'll never forget how much care she took in helping me find my love of cooking.

My parents were busy growing our family food business into the global household brand they always hoped for, and I spent every holiday at the office learning the tricks of the trade. My mum would bring home recipes she had been experimenting with and test them out on my brothers and me. If we liked them, they would find their way into a jar and onto the supermarket shelf. My parents made sure we were exposed to a wide variety of flavors from all corners of the world, and little did I know that I was training my taste buds for a life in food.

"I grew up in a spice-loving family where spice not only dominated our dishes but was usually the topic of conversation around the table."

Spices are magical ingredients that have the ability to transform a dish from ordinary to extraordinary. Spices are big, bold and vibrant, exploding in your mouth and making you feel alive. Although this experience isn't for everyone, when I first tasted Indian food I was hooked and instantly understood that adding a few spices to some simple ingredients can create delicious results. I was lucky enough to eat incredible food at home. Coming from a whole generation of accomplished cooks, we loved to stay in, cook and then eat as a family rather than going out. Traditional Indian food made by my grandmother or experimental Asian cooking by my mum was what I regarded as the norm. When I left home to study at uni, I realized it was rare to have grown-up cooking at home to that creative level. Those early cooking lessons are ones I will cherish forever.

In putting this book together, I wanted to draw on the food I love and have loved growing up. The dishes I've included are all inspired by the special food encounters I've experienced and the wonderful flavors and ingredients I've discovered along the way. From our Sunday roast family favorite Slow-roast Spiced Lamb (*see* page 44) to my dad's Smokin' Ribs (*see* page 132), which we have only once a year, all my recipes hold a special place in my heart.

Throughout my life, and as a result of my travels and my experiences, my confidence in using spices has grown. My professional culinary training at Leiths School of Food and Wine in London taught me techniques I'd never used before, and I've embraced many new ingredients, flavors and ideas from around the world to help bring out the enchanting qualities of spices. I wanted to offer a good balance of recipes, between light, uplifting dishes that you can ease into your busy life, and a few long, slow-cooked ones designed to intensify those luscious Indian flavors. Here are recipes for those rushed days when cooking needs to be especially quick, along with showstoppers for sun-filled barbecues and dinner parties. I've also included plenty of nutritious, feel-good dishes for the health conscious. The Sugar & Spice section has the most recipes, as I have a sweet tooth just like my father and go crazy for desserts.

Scattered throughout the recipes are My Secret stamps giving you tips on how to make the most of your ingredients, ways to tweak the recipes for slightly different yet still scrumptious results, and some of my favorite serving suggestions. I also simply had to share some of my secret kitchen essentials with you, including a peek into my Everyday Spice Box (*see* pages 37–41) and Pantry Must-Haves (*see* pages 68–69), which

"The best recipes only taste the best because they are filled with emotion, filled with love. They come from precious memories, and all have a story to tell."

"This book isn't for those wanting to learn traditional Indian cooking, but for those who love the spice flavors characteristic of Indian food and want to be shown how to use them in exciting and unexpected ways."

Kitchen Gadgets I rely on (*see* pages 110–11), how to make the most of Magical Chiles (*see* pages 88–89) and my Wine & Spice guide (*see* pages 214–15).

Indian food is usually seen as complicated with seemingly endless ingredient lists, but I wanted to share recipes with you that won't take forever and don't need a truckload of ingredients. A well-stocked pantry is all you need, and if you don't have one of the items listed, don't worry about it—simply leave it out, use your intuition and the end result will taste great.

I'm particularly passionate about bringing out the cook and food lover within each and every one of us, and I have sought to feature recipes that will both inspire those who love to cook as well as entice and satisfy those who love to eat. I want my recipes to be used as a canvas for experimenting with flavors. That's the way I love to cook, with my pantry wide open so that I can see what I have to play with. But my desire to eat well will always lead my taste buds back to the spice flavors of home, and my family who helped me discover my great love of food.

"I believe that cooking should be a pleasurable experience and approached with an adventurous mind."

I have always believed that good cookbooks should be covered in splashes from the preparation of meals gone by, and full of the cook's own scribbled substitutions and suggestions. They should look dog-eared and crinkled from being well read and frequently cooked from. That's what I hope for my cookbook . . . a book that is loved and used for many years to come.

CHAPTER

1

LIGHT BITES

SERVES 4
(MAKES ABOUT 12)
Prep time 10 minutes
Cook time 5 minutes if
cooking in a single batch

vegetable oil, for frying—you won't
    need more than 1 quart
2 carrots
1 large red onion
1¼-inch piece fresh ginger,
    peeled
good handful of spinach leaves,
    roughly chopped
1 red chile, finely chopped
2 tbsp roughly chopped
    fresh cilantro

1 tsp cumin seeds
1 tsp ground turmeric
1 tsp garam masala
½ tsp ground asafetida/hing
    (see page 41) (optional)
juice of 1 lemon
good pinch of sea salt
¾ cup gram (chickpea) flour
    (see My Secret, below)

Carrot, onion & spinach bhajias

Bhajias will always hold a special place in my heart. When my grandparents moved to the UK in the 1950s they were incredibly poor, so they had to do whatever they could to keep themselves afloat and provide for my dad and his siblings. My grandmother did what she loved, which was cooking. Her Indian samosas, bhajias and traditional desserts gained national fame, and from these humble beginnings the Patak's brand was born. My granny loved being in the kitchen and she taught me more about Gujarati cooking than I could ever thank her for. This is actually not one of her recipes but more of a modern spin on an old classic.

Pour vegetable oil into a large, deep-lipped skillet so that it comes 2 inches up the sides. Gently heat it while you prepare the bhajia mixture. Alternatively, heat a deep-fat fryer to 350°F.

Grate the carrots, onion and ginger using a cheese grater. Transfer them to a large bowl and add the rest of the ingredients. Scrunch all of the mixture together with your hands to release the moisture from the veggies and help it bind together. If you need to, add a few tablespoons of water—you want it to be a dropping consistency. Shape the mixture into balls of around a tablespoonful each before flattening them a little, which allows them to cook all the way through so that they don't end up with a doughy center.

Add a little of the mixture to the oil to test if it's hot enough: it should sink and then swim. Deep-fry the bhajias, in batches if you need to, for about 5 minutes until they are golden brown. You will need to flip them a few times to get an even color. Drain on paper towels.

Serve hot with Mango Chutney (see page 167) or your favorite dip.

· MY SECRET ·
Gram flour, made from ground chickpeas, is used widely in Indian cooking and is gluten free. It can be found in most supermarkets. If you don't have any at hand, use all-purpose flour instead and add a little more turmeric to give the bhajias a good color.

SERVES 4
Prep time 20 minutes
Cook time 5 minutes

Stuffing
3 tbsp ricotta cheese
1 garlic clove, finely chopped
1/2 tbsp finely chopped chives
1/2 tbsp pine nuts, toasted and finely
    chopped, plus extra to garnish
pinch of ground green
    cardamom (optional)

8 zucchini flowers with baby
    zucchini attached (preferably),
    flower stamens removed
2 tbsp vegetable oil
good drizzle of honey
1 fresh red chile, seeded and
    finely chopped

Stuffed zucchini flowers with ricotta & honey

Zucchini flowers are seen as exotic and are only available when zucchini come into season. They have a light, subtle flavor and so I'm adding sweet spices to my ricotta with just a little chile heat to help the honey taste even sweeter. This is a great starter to any meal.

Mix all the stuffing ingredients together in a bowl.

Slit the zucchini through the middle lengthwise but not all the way to the top so that the heat from the pan can cook them all the way through. Carefully stuff the flowers with the ricotta stuffing, trying not to overfill them. Twist the top to seal.

Gently heat the oil in a large skillet and fry the flowers for a few minutes until they are light golden brown on all sides. Transfer the flowers to a plate, draining on paper towels if you need to, and drizzle with honey. Sprinkle over the chile and a few extra toasted pine nuts to garnish.

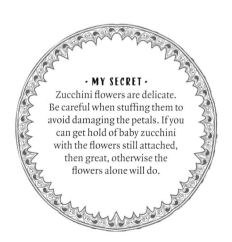

· MY SECRET ·
Zucchini flowers are delicate.
Be careful when stuffing them to
avoid damaging the petals. If you
can get hold of baby zucchini
with the flowers still attached,
then great, otherwise the
flowers alone will do.

SERVES 4 AS A SNACK
Prep time 5 minutes
Cook time 3 minutes if
cooking in a single batch

3 tbsp vegetable oil or light olive
   oil, plus extra if needed
8 oz okra, thinly sliced
2 tbsp gram (chickpea) flour
   or all-purpose flour
1 tsp ground turmeric
1/2 tsp chile powder
1 tbsp ground sumac
pinch of sea salt, or to taste

Crispy sumac okra

Frying okra makes this otherwise slimy vegetable taste absolutely wonderful. The sticky texture disappears and it becomes one of the best snacks you'll ever try. In India they would make a spice mix to dust on the okra before frying, but instead of following tradition I have opted for sumac as my flavoring of choice. It's a Middle Eastern spice made from beautiful dried crimson berries that have a sweet, sour and almost lemony flavor. Sumac is now widely available, but you can always substitute your favorite garam masala if you can't find it, although it doesn't have the same flavor. Try and cut the okra all the same size to ensure that they crisp up together without some of them burning.

Heat the oil in a large, shallow skillet. Sprinkle the okra with the flour, turmeric and chile powder, and toss together well so that they are all evenly coated.

Test the temperature of the oil by dropping in a little pinch of flour: it should sizzle. Add the okra to the pan and fry for a few minutes, moving them around frequently, until they are light golden brown and crispy. Be careful, as they burn easily, so turn down the heat if you need to. Depending on the size of your pan, you may need to do this in batches, so add a little more oil when frying each batch.

Drain on paper towels and sprinkle over the sumac with a good pinch of sea salt. Taste and adjust the flavorings if you need to. Serve hot with a chilled drink for a wonderful party snack.

· MY SECRET ·
I was always taught
never to wash okra,
as they absorb water,
so instead I wipe them
with a damp cloth
to clean them.

SERVES 4
Prep time 5 minutes
Cook time 15 minutes

10 baby eggplants, cut in half
and flesh scored with a cross
2 tbsp vegetable oil

Stuffing
2 tsp black mustard seeds
2 tsp peeled and finely chopped
fresh ginger
1–2 fresh red chiles, finely chopped

15 fresh curry leaves
4 heaped tbsp dried unsweetened
coconut
3 tbsp chopped chives
pinch of sea salt, or to taste

To finish
2 tbsp plain Greek yogurt
honey, for drizzling

Charred baby eggplants

My grandmother used to make a dish just like this when I was young. She used large eggplant but I prefer baby ones as they are just the right size for snacking when they are halved lengthwise. If you do use large ones, make sure you roast them for longer.

Preheat an outdoor grill to medium or the oven to 425°F. Rub the eggplants with half the oil and grill with the lid down or roast, cut-side down. The skin should start to change color and turn crispy after 10–15 minutes.

In the meantime, make the stuffing. Gently heat the remaining oil in a small skillet and add the mustard seeds. When the seeds start to jump out of the pan, add the ginger, chiles and curry leaves and allow to cook for 1 minute before stirring in the coconut. This should start to toast and turn golden brown after around 30 seconds. Turn off the heat and add half the chives and a pinch of salt. Stir well and taste and adjust the seasoning if you need to.

Remove the eggplants from the grill or oven and flip them over so that you can see the flesh side. Fill the aubergines with the stuffing. Drizzle with the yogurt and some honey, and sprinkle over the remaining chives before serving.

· MY SECRET ·
Fresh curry leaves must be thoroughly rinsed under cold running water before use. Available at Asian stores and large supermarkets, curry leaves freeze well. Buy a large bag to freeze for use whenever a recipe calls for them.

SERVES 4 AS A SNACK
Prep time 10 minutes
Cook time 5 minutes

14 oz cleaned squid, cut into
 small bite-size pieces
milk, for soaking
vegetable oil, for frying
5 tbsp all-purpose flour
1 tsp ajwain seeds (optional)
1/2 tsp ground turmeric
1/4 tsp ground asafetida/hing
 (*see* page 41) (optional)

sea salt and pepper
2 scallions, finely chopped
2 garlic cloves, finely chopped
1 fresh red chile, seeded if you
 wish, finely chopped
20 fresh curry leaves
 (*see* My Secret, page 20)
juice of 1 lime

Flash-fried calamari

Fried squid wins the hearts of most people and I'm one of them. As much as I like the usual sprinkling of salt and citrus, I'm going for something different here. I've fried up some scallions, garlic, chile and curry leaves to toss through, and it tastes awesome!

I'm using the tried-and-trusted tenderizing technique of soaking the squid in milk. It tastes best if you can leave it for a few hours, but in this recipe I only do it for 5 minutes while I get on with the chopping. Something is better than nothing.

Soak the squid in milk, making sure it is completely covered, while you prepare the other ingredients.

Pour vegetable oil into a large, deep-lipped skillet so that it comes 3/4 inch up the sides and put on to heat. Alternatively, heat a deep-fat fryer to 400°F.

Put the flour in a large bowl and stir in the ajwain seeds (if using), turmeric, asafetida/hing (if using) and a really good pinch of salt and pepper. Drain the squid and toss in the flour mixture.

Test the temperature of the oil by dropping in a little pinch of flour: it should sizzle. Once the oil is hot enough, dust off any excess flour and carefully deep-fry the squid, in batches, for 1 minute—any longer and it will be rubbery. Drain on paper towels.

In the meantime, prepare the flavorings to sprinkle over the calamari. Gently heat 1 tablespoon vegetable oil in a small skillet, stir in the scallions, garlic, chile and curry leaves and fry for 1 minute.

Spoon the fried mixture all over the hot calamari, squeeze over the lime juice and sprinkle with a little more salt before serving.

Mini tortillas

Now I know this is a Mexican classic, but who doesn't love tortillas? And I couldn't write a cookbook without including some of my favorite recipes. I've used store-bought tortilla wraps here, but you can make your own if you like, and they aren't that difficult to do. I actually prefer the ready-made ones.

These are some of my favorite tortilla fillings. Make just one or cook them all up, pile separate bowls in the middle of the table and top your tortillas with whatever you like. Sprinkle with finely sliced red onions, jalapeños and some sour cream or yogurt for a true feast. Roll up and devour: no cutlery allowed!

Prep time 10 minutes
Cook time 1½ hours for chicken, or up to 3 hours for pork

1 onion, sliced
2 Indian bay leaves
6 bone-in chicken thighs, skin removed, or 1 lb boneless pork shoulder, skin and all the fat removed
2 tbsp tomato paste
1 tbsp ketchup or barbecue sauce
1 tbsp chipotle paste or canned chopped chipotle chiles (use less if you don't like it fiery)
2 garlic cloves, finely chopped
1 tbsp light brown sugar
2 tsp smoked paprika
juice of 1 orange
1 cup chicken or vegetable stock

Pulled chicken or pork

Preheat the oven to 300°F.

Lay the onion and bay leaves in the base of a small roasting tray, one that will fit the chicken or pork snugly. Place the meat on top.

Make the marinade by mixing together all the remaining ingredients. Pour over the meat, cover tightly with foil and slow cook in the oven for about 90 minutes for chicken, or up to 3 hours for pork, basting the meat every now and again, until cooked through and falling off the bone.

Shred the meat and mix into the sauce (discard the bay leaves). If the sauce isn't thick enough, you can put the meat aside to keep warm while you reduce it in a saucepan over medium-high heat.

Roast corn salsa

Prep time 10 minutes
Cook time 10 minutes

1 tbsp vegetable oil
7 oz corn, drained if canned or
    defrosted if frozen
1 tsp cumin seeds
2 garlic cloves, finely chopped
1 fresh red chile, seeded if you
    wish, sliced
1 scallion, finely sliced
good pinch of sea salt, or to taste
grated zest and juice of 1 lime
3 cherry tomatoes, cut into
    quarters (optional)
chopped mint, to garnish

Gently heat a large skillet, add the oil and corn, and give it a good stir. Turn up the heat and allow the corn to cook until golden brown. Be careful, as the kernels will start to jump out of the pan.

Stir in the cumin seeds, garlic, chile, scallion, salt and the lime juice. Allow to cook for a few minutes before stirring in the tomatoes (if using).

Taste and adjust the seasoning if you need to, then garnish with the lime zest and mint.

Avocado & cilantro salsa

Prep time 5 minutes

2 ripe avocados, peeled, pitted
    and mashed lightly with a fork
juice of 1/2 lime
1 scallion, roughly chopped
1 fresh red chile, seeded and
    finely chopped
1 tbsp roughly chopped cilantro
good pinch of sea salt
crumbled feta cheese,
    to garnish (optional)

Mix all the ingredients together in a serving bowl and top with a little feta cheese (if using), in which case, remember to go easy on the salt, as the feta will be salty.

Chickpea salsa

Prep time 10 minutes

1/2 15-oz can chickpeas, drained
2 tbsp light olive oil
1 fresh Indian finger chile or
    jalapeño, roughly chopped
1 roasted red pepper, seeded and
    roughly chopped
1 tbsp roughly chopped cilantro
1 tbsp roughly chopped mint
1 tsp coriander seeds, toasted
    (*see* page 38) (optional)
1/2 red onion, roughly chopped
good pinch of sea salt, or to taste
juice of 1/2 lime, or to taste

Place all the ingredients in a food processor and pulse a few times until almost smooth—add some water if you need to. Taste and adjust the seasoning.

SERVES 4
Prep time 5 minutes, plus
(preferably) marinating
Cook time 35–40 minutes

12 chicken wings

Hot pepper marinade
2 dried red chiles or a good
   pinch of chile powder
1 tsp fennel seeds
1 tsp cumin seeds
1 tsp coriander seeds
1 tsp black peppercorns
1 tbsp peeled and roughly
   chopped fresh ginger
2 garlic cloves, peeled
1 scallion, roughly chopped
1 tbsp tamarind paste

1/2 tbsp honey
good pinch of ground cinnamon
good pinch of sea salt
1 tbsp vegetable oil

Tandoori marinade
4 tbsp plain Greek yogurt
1 tbsp garlic paste
2 tsp ginger paste
1 tsp ground turmeric
1/2–1 tsp chile powder
2 tsp garam masala
good pinch of sea salt

Spiced chicken wings

My love for wings comes from many school holidays spent in the US visiting family. We would eat them nearly every day—which sounds excessive but we absolutely loved them. This isn't a shy dish, so roll up your sleeves and get stuck in. These two versions of spiced wings really are finger-licking good. Tone down the heat or dial it up, depending on what you feel like.

I spent some time learning the regional cuisine in an area of South India called Chettinad. This Hot Pepper Marinade is inspired by my travels, and it's aromatic and punchy with a good hit of spice. I've added one of my favorite ingredients, tamarind, but you can leave it out if you haven't got any.

Hot pepper wings

For the hot pepper marinade, gently heat a heavy-bottomed skillet and toast the dry spices for a few minutes until fragrant and the seeds are golden brown.

Transfer to a mortar and allow to cool for a few minutes, then roughly grind with a pestle. Add the ginger, garlic and scallion, and bash together to form a paste. Toss in the rest of the ingredients and taste—the marinade should be slightly sweet, sour and full of flavor.

Rub the marinade over the wings in a dish, cover and leave to marinate in the fridge for a few hours if you can.

Preheat the oven to 400°F and heat up a griddle pan, if you have one, or a cast-iron skillet, over a medium heat. This will get a nice char on the wings before you pop them in the oven to fully cook through.

Char-grill the wings in the griddle pan for a few minutes on each side before transferring to the oven and cooking for a further 30 minutes, or a few minutes longer if not char-grilled. Check they are cooked through before diving in and serving with a relish (*see* pages 162–63).

Tandoori wings

Mix all the ingredients for the tandoori marinade together and rub all over the wings in a dish. Marinate, cook and serve as above.

My grandfather (right) Lakshmishankar, fondly known as LG, or Bapuji to me, with Dhiru Mama, Baa's brother (center), at 134 Drummond Street, London. Indians from all over would travel to the capital to stock up on Bapuji's imported spices, lentils, rices, pulses and homemade Bombay mix. Demand and community spirit were high.

My grandmother (right) Shanta, respectfully known as Baa, cooking up yet another batch of her famous jalebis. Queues for Baa's authentic sweets were long. My dad and his brothers were soon kept busy delivering parcels all over London (making the most of the free Tube travel for Under 11's).

Baa at Allcroft Road, Kentish Town—this was the first home Baa and Bapuji rented upon arriving in London from Kenya in 1956. Baa would cook up sweets in the tiny kitchen here, sales of which led to the opening of the Drummond Street grocery store. Thus, Patak's was born.

Baa (pictured) and Bapuji invest in a van to keep up with delivery demands following the opening of the Drummond Street store!

Dad takes a break from making deliveries to pose with his beloved guitar.

SERVES 4
(MAKES ABOUT 16)
Prep time 10 minutes
Cook time 25 minutes

1/4 lb potatoes (any variety), roughly chopped into small pieces
1 tsp ground turmeric
sea salt
1/2 lb puff pastry, 1/4 inch thick, cut into 16 disks about 2 inches in diameter
1 tbsp vegetable oil
1 tsp black mustard seeds
1/4 tsp ground asafetida/hing (see page 41) (optional)
1 fresh red chile, seeded if you wish, finely chopped

1 tsp garam masala
juice of 1/2 lemon

Topping
1 tsp cumin seeds
4 tbsp plain Greek yogurt
4 tbsp Sticky Sweet Date Chutney (see page 168)
1/2 small red onion, finely chopped
2 tbsp roughly chopped cilantro
seeds of 1 pomegranate (optional)
2 tbsp sev (see headnote) (optional)

Papri chaat

Chaat is the name of a whole host of dishes that are eaten on the streets of India. They are utterly delicious and can vary from one street vendor to the next. This is my recipe for papri chaat, which is traditionally made with potatoes and chickpeas and smothered in yogurt, something sweet and salty (often Sticky Sweet Date Chutney—see page 168) and some crispy gram noodles called sev. All of this sits on cute little fried pastry disks that can be served warm or cold. To make it authentic is quite tricky, especially if you don't have all the ingredients, so I've made a few shortcuts. For instance, life is too short to make your own pastry and so I have used the store-bought variety, but by all means make your own.

Preheat the oven to 400°F.

Fill a saucepan with cold water, add the potatoes with half the turmeric and some salt and bring to a boil. Cook until soft (around 10 minutes). Once cooked, drain well.

In the meantime, lay the pastry disks on a baking sheet lined with parchment paper. Place another sheet of parchment paper and a baking sheet on top to stop them puffing up. Bake until golden brown on both sides (around 10 minutes). Keep an eye on them, as they color quickly.

Heat the oil in a saucepan and add the mustard seeds, asafetida/hing (if using) and the remaining turmeric. Once sizzling, stir in the chile, cooked potatoes, and garam masala. Using a fork, roughly mash the potatoes into the spices. Squeeze over the lemon juice and season with a pinch of salt. After a few minutes the spices will have cooked through, so give it a taste and adjust the seasoning.

Put the potatoes to one side to cool a little, and also allow the puff pastry disks to cool down before putting it all together.

Gently heat a heavy-bottomed skillet and toast the cumin seeds for a few minutes until golden brown and fragrant. Pour into a mortar, allow to cool for a few minutes, then roughly crush with a pestle.

Start by laying out the puff pastry disks. Top with a heaped teaspoon of the spiced potato and then a good dollop of the yogurt and chutney. Scatter over the onion, cilantro, pomegranate seeds and sev (if using), and add a good sprinkling of the toasted cumin.

SERVES 4 AS A SNACK
Prep time 10 minutes
Cook time 10 minutes

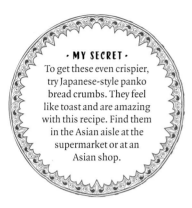

Tomato chutney
3 large tomatoes or 20 cherry
   tomatoes, roughly chopped
1/2 red onion, finely chopped
good pinch of kalonji (black onion
   or nigella) seeds (optional)
15 fresh curry leaves
   (*see* My Secret, page 20)
   (optional)
good pinch of crushed red pepper
   flakes or chile powder
1 tbsp light brown sugar
1 tsp red wine vinegar
good pinch of sea salt, or to taste

2 garlic cloves, peeled
2 tbsp pine nuts
1 tbsp basil leaves
1 tbsp freshly grated Parmesan
   cheese
1 tsp peeled and roughly chopped
   fresh ginger
1 fresh red chile, seeded if you wish
1/2 tsp cumin seeds, toasted
   (*see* page 171) (optional)
juice of 1/2 lemon
1 pack paneer, around 8 oz
1 small naan bread—any flavor,
   but I like garlic and coriander
1 egg, beaten
2 tbsp vegetable oil or light olive oil

Stuffed paneer bites

These are a wonderful snack to have when you fancy something a little naughty. I'm not a big fan of paneer, which is the cheese most commonly used in Indian dishes, but when it's fried, all that changes. It doesn't melt like other cheese but rather softens, and its neutral flavor makes it one of the most versatile ingredients around. Here I have made a stuffing quite similar to a pimped-up pesto and then rolled it in bread crumbs, which I make from slightly stale naan bread; but you can use ordinary white bread instead. It tastes best when served with a chutney, so try this simple fresh tomato one if you have time.

Gently heat all the tomato chutney ingredients together in a saucepan for 10 minutes. Add a splash of water if it starts to dry out, but allow it to thicken.

In the meantime, prepare the paneer bites. Make the stuffing for the paneer by using a food processor to finely chop together the garlic, pine nuts, basil, Parmesan, ginger, chile and cumin with the lemon juice (or chop very fine with a knife and mix together). Give it a taste and adjust the seasoning if you think it needs it.

Cut the paneer in half as if you are about to make a sandwich. Spread the stuffing on top of one layer and put the other paneer layer on top. Cut it into large bite-size pieces.

Make the bread crumbs by pulsing the naan in the food processor, or grate on a cheese grater, and put into a bowl.

Dip the paneer bites into the beaten egg in a bowl and then into the bread crumbs. Gently heat the oil in a large skillet and fry the paneer bites for a minute or so on each side until light golden brown and crispy. Drain on paper towels. Serve them piled high with the tomato chutney.

SERVES 4 AS A SNACK
Prep time 5 minutes
Cook time 20 minutes

$10^1/_2$ oz unsalted mixed nuts
1 egg white, beaten until frothy
4 tbsp light brown sugar
1 tsp smoked paprika
1 tsp ground cinnamon

1–2 tsp chile powder
2 tsp salt—I love sea salt
20 fresh curry leaves
   (*see* My Secret, page 20)
   (optional)

Bombay nuts

Nuts are the ultimate snack and even more so when dusted with spices, sugar and salt. Serve these at your next party and you'll be hearing praises all night! Sweet, salty, hot and smoky . . . the best combo.

Preheat the oven to 325°F and cover a large rimmed baking sheet with parchment paper.

Mix the nuts with the egg white in a bowl and make sure the nuts are all coated well.

In a separate small bowl, stir together the sugar, spices and salt, then sprinkle over the nuts. Add the curry leaves (if using) and toss together before transferring the nuts to the lined baking sheet. Spread them out in a single layer.

Bake in the oven for 20 minutes, stirring them halfway through. Leave to cool on the baking sheet before breaking them apart and serving. They taste best warm.

SERVES 4
Prep time 10 minutes
Cook time 10 minutes

2 tbsp vegetable oil
1 cinnamon stick
1 tsp black mustard seeds
1 tsp ground turmeric
$1/2$ tsp black peppercorns, crushed
   with a pestle and mortar
20 fresh curry leaves
   (*see* My Secret, page 20)
   (optional)
2 scallions, finely sliced

1 fresh red chile, finely sliced
1 tbsp peeled and julienned
   fresh ginger
20 raw jumbo shrimp, shells
   removed but tails left on,
   deveined
good pinch of sea salt
good drizzle of honey
2 tbsp roughly chopped cilantro
juice of $1/2$ lime, to taste

Tiger shrimp with lime, ginger & mustard seeds

Shrimp are quick to cook and somehow feel rather exotic. This recipe borrows spices from the southern shores of India and I tasted a dish similar to this when I was learning about the local cuisine. My mouth was on fire with the chiles, but when I got past it I found the flavor to be delicate and delicious. I have toned down the chiles and added some background warmth by using fresh ginger instead.

I've used tiger shrimp and removed most of the shell, apart from the tail. I prefer to leave the tail on, as it means that you have something to hold on to when biting into the shrimp, but you can take the entire shell off if you prefer. Just make sure the shrimp are raw and that they have been deveined.

Gently heat the oil in a large skillet and add the cinnamon stick, mustard seeds, turmeric, peppercorns and curry leaves (if using). Once they start to sizzle, stir through the scallions, chile and ginger and allow to soften for around a minute.

Stir in the shrimp and watch how they turn to a golden pink color. Flip them over and sprinkle over a good pinch of salt. Once they are cooked through—and it won't take long, only a few minutes on each side—drizzle over the honey and sprinkle in half the cilantro and the lime juice. Mix well and serve sprinkled with the remaining cilantro.

Everyday spice box

Spices are the life and soul of all Indian dishes and are the ingredients that make your taste buds come to life. They brighten up even the simplest dishes by adding a little magic. As a little girl I would wander into the kitchen to see what wonderful dishes my family was creating as the scents wafted through the house. I came across my mum's spice box, which was the most amazing, colorful thing I'd ever seen. The smells were incredible but what surprised me most was the sheer amount she had crammed in there. As I grew up I learned how to use these little potent wonders and I've been hooked ever since.

Each Indian family will fill their spice box with their favorite spices; some will even have two or three boxes, depending how adventurously the family cooks. I like to keep one everyday box that contains most of the spices I need from all corners of India. I say "most" because I can't quite fit every single spice from my pantry in there and if I want my dish to taste typically southern, for example, then I need to add a few extras. I have two layers to it—my base layer filled with canisters of spices, and then the top layer packed with a mix of aromatic spices.

Buying super-fresh spices is a bit of an art, and something my father taught me. Spices have always been very special to him, not only as they were at the heart of our spice business, but he met my mum on one of his spice buying trips to India. Some spices are robust and don't lose much flavor as they age, while others need to be bought as fresh as can be so they deliver the best possible flavor punch. Have you ever wondered why recipes taste different every time you cook them, even though you've made them the exact same way? It's down to the quality of your ingredients. If you hold on to spices for years, you will never have a fresh-tasting dish as your core ingredients will have changed and lost their beautiful essence. I know buying fresh spices isn't always possible, not to mention affordable, so here are a few tips on how to buy and store my favorite spices that I keep in my everyday spice box.

Base-layer spices

CORIANDER SEEDS
These seeds are one of the most important spices in my box. Coriander is one of the only spices that can be used throughout the recipe—seeds at the beginning, powder a little later on, and finished with the fresh leaf (cilantro). I absolutely love the earthy lemony flavor it imparts in a dish and it is the perfect spice to create a good flavor base. The seeds can be toasted in a dry pan to help release their sweet flavor, and I like to sprinkle them on top of dishes to add a little mystery. Look for darkish beige-brown plump seeds. They turn light beige as they get older. Try with Tomato & Red Onion Salad with Toasted Coriander & Burrata (*see* page 84).

CUMIN SEEDS
I love love love cumin seeds. They help create a good flavor base, add a warm earthy note to dishes, and taste incredible when toasted and ground. Not to be confused with black cumin or royal cumin, which adds a very different flavor. Buy cumin seeds when they are brown, plump and unbroken. Try with Lentil Salad with Toasted Cumin

Dressing or Cumin Roast Potatoes (*see* pages 96 and 146).

TURMERIC
A very special spice that doesn't seem to age. I call it the "wonder" spice simply because it is truly wonderful. It has a unique healing ability, which acts as a natural cleanser, drawing impurities out of everything it comes into contact with, which is why it is used to heal the body externally as well as internally. It's a member of the ginger family and looks slightly similar in appearance. It has an orangey yellow skin and is much smaller than fresh ginger, with bright orange flesh inside. If you can get your hands on fresh turmeric then you can pop it in the freezer, otherwise the more common form is dried and ground. Its yellow color stains every single thing it touches and it can taste very bitter when raw, so I like to cook it well to bring out its slightly sweet flavor. Try with Scented Steamed Fish (*see* page 124).

BLACK PEPPER
Once known as the King of the Spices, it used to be one of the most expensive spices in the world and has a rich history. Unlike in the West where it is only used

as a seasoning, in India cooks use black pepper as a spice in its own right. Black pepper is surprisingly warm and brings a lot of heat to dishes. Buy dark black wrinkly peppercorns that are as whole as possible; they lose their flavor very quickly once ground. Try with Chile Beef with Black Pepper (see page 60).

BLACK MUSTARD SEEDS
These tiny brown/black seeds add warmth and a slightly nutty flavor to dishes. They can be ground, made into a paste, used to flavor oil (mustard oil is very pungent), or used whole. They come in different sizes, and hold their flavor well as they age, so look out for dark-colored seeds and whatever you do try not to drop the tub on the floor—they spread everywhere! Try with Wilted Mustard Greens (see page 158).

CHILE POWDER
Chiles gained fame in India only a few centuries ago. Before that it was black pepper that was known for being the heat-infusing ingredient. Chile powder can vary in heat level and it is only ever red as fresh green chiles can't be dried naturally. Bright deep-red chile powder carries less heat and is made from Kashmiri red chiles, but the only way to tell how hot your chile powder is, is to taste it! The dried seeds from dried red chiles can be used to add more heat, or leave them out if you want a milder chile powder. Try with Flaky Mint & Chile Paratha (see page 149).

GARAM MASALA
The myth with garam masala is that it can only ever be one recipe. In truth, each cook will have his or her own recipe for garam masala, usually passed down from mother to daughter, and may even have several masalas as each one works best with different dishes. My garam masala recipe was given to me by my mum and it is very precious to me. You can buy good garam masalas off the shelf, but there is nothing like making it fresh as ground masalas lose their potency quickly. Lightly toast whole spices (never turmeric) until fragrant and warm before tipping into a spice grinder. It can be a blend of anything from two spices up to fifty spices, whatever the cook wants it to be. Try with Crunchy Roast Cauliflower & Broccoli (see page 145).

Top-layer spices

INDIAN BAY LEAVES
Indian bay leaves can't be substituted
for European bay leaves as they have a
different flavor, so leave them out if
you don't have dried Indian bay leaves.
If you're unsure what type yours are
simply rub the leaves with your
fingertips—if you can smell a hint of
cinnamon then they are fine to use.
Avoid buying leaves that are discolored
and holey. Try with One-Pot Chicken
with Smoked Spices (*see* page 46).

CINNAMON STICKS
I love cinnamon and prefer to buy the
sticks as I can seek it out during cooking
should I need to remove it. Its sweet,
mesmerizing flavor is best when whole
and is lost quickly once ground into a fine
powder. Try with Tadka Dhal (*see* page 154).

GREEN CARDAMOM
If black pepper is the King of the Spices
then this is its queen. Buy bright dark-
green pods that aren't too shriveled as the
black seeds inside hold all the flavor.
Green cardamom has a sweet camphor,
almost aniseed, flavor and is by far my
favorite spice. My first spice-buying trip
to India led me to a cardamom auction

and I fell in love with this beautiful spice.
Try with Roast Hazelnut & Cardamom
Ice Cream (*see* page 176).

BLACK CARDAMOM
Although part of the same family as
green cardamom, black cardamom is
twice the size and more wrinkly, with a
smoky aroma from being toasted on hot
embers. Look out for large black dried
pods that smell very smoky. Try with
Black Dhal (*see* page 140).

MACE
This is the outer red lacy casing wrapped
around fresh nutmeg. Mace turns
orangey once dried and tastes almost
perfumey with a gentle floral backnote.
Look for whole pieces of mace that smell
floral. Try with Foolproof Pilau Rice (*see*
page 148).

CLOVES
Cloves have a medicinal flavor and cause a
distinctive numbing sensation if chewed.
You can tell they are fresh when they look
plump and are a deep dark brown and
almost black. The round heads should
still be attached to their long stems and
they should smell very strong. Try with
Roast Stone Fruit & Honey with Pistachio
Cream (*see* page 194).

STAR ANISE

This spice originally came from China but is now used in so many other cuisines across the world. It is by far the prettiest spice but its strong anise flavor can overpower a recipe so don't go too crazy. Look for large stars that have their pods still nestled in between the points. Try with Pineapple Anise Colada (*see* page 209).

SAFFRON

Although I don't keep saffron in my spice box, I do keep it in its very own special tub next to my box. Saffron strands are the stigmas of a variety of crocus flowers that only open for a few weeks of the year. Each flower produces only three stigmas and they have to be handpicked at dawn before the suns rays burn them. It is the world's most expensive spice and has a unique and enchanting floral flavor and color. It's hard to know the quality of saffron without touching it and smelling it. Usually the more expensive it is, the better quality it will be. Try with Saffron & Honey Naan Breads or Saffron, Cardamom & Thyme Celery Root (*see* pages 156 and 158).

ASAFETIDA/HING

This is another spice I don't keep in my spice box, but it is an essential spice I keep in my pantry in an airtight container. It usually comes in a powder, but you can find it in its raw state as a dried resin that looks like a rock made from amber-colored glass. I secretly love its strong, pungent smell and use it as a flavor enhancer; when cooked in oil, it tastes like garlic and fried onions. Sprinkle it in Carrot, Onion & Spinach Bhajias (see page 14). You can't really substitute the flavor of asafetida, but you could use extra garlic if you can't find it.

Storing & using your spices

Always keep your spices in an airtight container. A spice box is perfect. Oxygen and sunlight age your spices quickly so try to keep them somewhere dark. When you grind spices to create powders you start to release their essential oils, their essence, which will then float off into the air as time goes on. Grinding your spices only as you need them will give you the best flavor so try to buy your spices whole and use them up quickly.

CHAPTER

BIG BITES

SERVES 6 TO 8
Prep time 30 minutes
Cook time 5 hours

Spice paste
1 tsp coriander seeds
2 tsp cumin seeds
2 tsp fennel seeds
1/2 tsp black peppercorns
1 tsp ground turmeric
2 tsp Creole mustard
4 tbsp vegetable oil

1 leg of lamb, about 4 1/2 lbs
5 garlic cloves, peeled, 2 for the
    Spice Paste
4 rosemary sprigs, cut into
    small pieces
2 tbsp mint leaves
1 fresh red chile, seeded if you
    wish, sliced
2 onions, finely sliced
sea salt
2 1/4 cups hot lamb or vegetable
    stock or water
pepper

· MY SECRET ·
Short on time? Buy a
butterflied leg and stud the
fleshy side with herbs and spices.
Cook skin-side up in a searingly hot
oven for 15 minutes, reduce the
temperature to 425°F and cook
for 30 minutes. Your lamb
will be beautifully pink.

Slow-roast spiced lamb

Another Sunday lunch favorite in my home when I was growing up, this recipe is one I cook regularly when I have friends coming around. Making a simple spice paste to rub over the lamb infuses the meat while it roasts, and just in case there isn't enough flavor going on, I stud the lamb with herbs and garlic. The juices that sit in the roasting tray are perfect for gravy, which I prefer thin and unadulterated, but you can add some flour to thicken it if you prefer.

Low and slow is what makes the meat meltingly tender. It will taste even better if you can roast it at a lower temperature. For every 25°F lower, add on an extra hour of cooking time. By the time it's ready, you won't even need a knife.

Make the spice paste by bashing up the coriander, cumin and fennel seeds with the peppercorns and 2 of the garlic cloves in a mortar with a pestle. Stir in the turmeric, mustard and oil, and mix well.

Preheat the oven to 275°F. Make some deep cuts into the meat at evenly spaced intervals and poke a finger in the cuts to check that they are wide enough for the herbs and spices.

Slice the remaining garlic cloves for stuffing into the holes in the lamb. Rub the spice paste all over the lamb, making sure you get some into the holes. Fill the holes with the rosemary, mint, chile and sliced garlic.

Toss the onions into a deep roasting tray, one that will fit the lamb snugly. Season the lamb well with salt and place on top. Pour in the hot stock or water, cover with foil and slow roast in the oven for 5 hours. Baste every hour with the spiced stock.

Remove from the oven and carefully place the lamb on a plate, cover with foil and leave to rest. The meat should be falling off the bone. Transfer the spiced stock to a saucepan (this is your gravy) and skim off any fat. Boil until reduced and thickened to your liking. Taste and adjust the seasoning with salt and pepper before serving with your slow-roast spiced lamb and maybe some Glazed Baby Potatoes (*see page 116*).

SERVES 4
Prep time 10 minutes
Cook time 1 hour

2 tbsp olive oil
3 Indian bay leaves
2 cinnamon sticks
2 onions, finely sliced
1/4 lb pancetta or smoked bacon,
    cut into small pieces
2 portobello mushrooms,
    trimmed and sliced
3 garlic cloves, finely sliced
4 chiles, 2 sliced and 2 stabbed
    with a knife

8 chicken joints—a mix of thighs
    and drumsticks
1 14-oz can chopped tomatoes,
    or 14 oz fresh tomatoes, chopped
1 quart chicken stock
1/2 lb new potatoes, cut in half
2 tbsp smoked paprika
1 tbsp garam masala
small bunch of cilantro

One-pot chicken with smoked spices

*One-pot cooking is my ideal
style of cooking—hardly any
washing up and it usually
doesn't involve too much
effort. This is one of my dinner
party favorites. After the
chopping is done and you've
started getting the flavors
going, you simply move it to
the oven and let it cook slowly.
If anyone turns up late, then
the chicken can sit happily
bubbling away until you
need it. Now that's what
I call relaxed entertaining.*

Preheat the oven to 350°F.

Gently heat the oil in a large flameproof casserole dish, or other large pan that can go in the oven, and add the bay leaves and cinnamon sticks. After a minute, add the onions and allow to soften for 5 minutes over medium-low heat. Stir in the pancetta or bacon and cook for 5 minutes, until the pancetta is crispy and the onions are golden brown. Stir in the mushrooms, garlic and chiles and allow to cook for 1 minute.

Add the chicken pieces, skin-side down, trying to fit them all in a single layer, as you want to crisp up the skin for a few minutes. Once the skin is golden brown, turn the chicken over and pour in the tomatoes, stock, potatoes, smoked paprika and garam masala. Cut the stalks off the cilantro and finely chop them. Add the chopped stalks to the pan and give everything a good stir. Cover the pan with a lid (or with foil if you haven't got a lid) and transfer to the oven to finish cooking through. The chicken will be ready after 40 minutes.

Carefully remove the lid and push the chicken to the surface so that the skin is above the tomato sauce. Turn the oven to broil and broil for a few minutes to allow the skin to turn crispy. In the meantime, roughly chop the cilantro leaves. Sprinkle over before serving with some Wilted Mustard Greens (*see* page 158).

· MY SECRET ·
For a vegetarian version,
add 1 pound soaked, cooked
and drained (or drained
canned) chickpeas instead of
chicken, leave out the bacon
and use veggie not chicken
stock. It tastes delicious.

SERVES 4
Prep time 15 minutes
Cook time 12 minutes

1/3 cup white long-grain rice—I like
    basmati
about 1/4 cup light brown sugar
2 oz English Breakfast tea leaves
2 cinnamon sticks
2 tsp fennel seeds
8 cloves
1 tsp ground green cardamom
8 skin-on sea bass fillets,
    scaled and pin-boned

Marinade
2 tsp fennel seeds
3 garlic cloves, peeled
1 tbsp peeled and roughly
    chopped fresh ginger
1–2 dried fresh red chiles
3 tbsp roughly chopped cilantro
juice of 1 lemon or lime
2 tsp honey
good pinch of sea salt, or to taste

Chai-smoked bass

Steaming fish using tea leaves is an old Chinese tradition, so I've borrowed the technique and added some of my favorite chai spices to the leaves during smoking. You need to add sugar to the leaves to help the tea smoke, and the rice keeps the tea burning longer. I'm using sea bass fillets here, with all the bones removed to make it easier to eat, but you can use whole fish instead—just make sure they've been well cleaned and gutted and their scales have been removed.

You need plenty of foil for this recipe and I like to put my fish on parchment paper so that the skin doesn't stick. I'm using loose English Breakfast tea, but you can always snip the top off a few tea bags and empty out the leaves.

Mix the rice, sugar and tea leaves together. Make the chai spice mix by roughly crushing the cinnamon sticks, fennel seeds and cloves using a pestle and mortar—they will release more flavor if they are broken up. Add them to the rice mixture and stir in the cardamom.

Line a large, heavy-bottomed saucepan, or large, heavy roasting tray, with 2 sheets of foil. Toss the rice mixture onto the foil and spread evenly over the base. Cover loosely with another piece of foil, making sure some smoke can escape, and place a steamer basket or rack on top. Cover with a lid, or foil, place the pan or tray on the stovetop and turn the heat to medium. Prepare the fish while you get the smoke going.

For the marinade, crush the fennel seeds with the pestle and mortar. Add the garlic, ginger, chiles and cilantro, and bash together. Mix in the lemon or lime juice, honey and a good pinch of salt. Rub the marinade all over the fish fillets (or inside and out if using whole fish).

Lay 4 fish fillets, skin-side down, on a piece of parchment paper and top with the other 4 fillets, skin-side up. Now you're ready to smoke the fish. Carefully lift the lid off the pan, or foil off the tray—it should have started to smoke by now—and place the fish on the paper on top of the steamer or rack. Put the lid, or foil, back on and cook for 10 to 12 minutes (or, if using an ovenproof pan, place in an oven preheated to 400°F). If you see smoke escaping, fit some foil tightly onto the rim of the pan.

Once cooked, remove the fish from the steamer or rack and serve with a lightly dressed salad.

SERVES 4
Prep time 10 minutes
Cook time 40 minutes

· MY SECRET ·
To cook the perfect steak,
make sure your pan is really hot
and don't add any oil. Oil your meat
instead with the spice marinade,
and try to get a good "bark" (those
charred bits) before flipping it over.
It will add bags of flavor. Make
sure you allow your meat to rest
before cutting into it.

Wedges
4 large baking potatoes, about
   1³/₄ lb, cut into wedges
2 tbsp light olive oil
2 tsp ground cumin
1 tsp smoked paprika
good pinch of sea salt and pepper
1 garlic head, cut in half horizontally

Steak marinade
2 tsp cumin seeds
¹/₄ tsp black peppercorns

¹/₂ tsp crushed red pepper flakes
1 tsp ground turmeric
2 garlic cloves, peeled
3 tbsp light olive oil
good pinch of sea salt

4 steaks, about 8 oz each—use any
   cut you prefer but make sure they
   are around 1¹/₂ inches thick and at
   room temperature
a few rosemary sprigs

Sizzling steak & cumin paprika wedges

There is nothing quite like tucking into a perfectly cooked steak with some fluffy crispy fries on the side—or wedges in this case. This is a wonderful recipe for those days when you want an easy meal with little cooking. Adding some spice to your steak gives it a different dimension and it means you don't need to make a sauce—all you need is a little horseradish and maybe some ketchup for dunking the wedges.

I can't stress enough how important the quality of the meat is, so buy the best you can. And if you're a garlic lover, then definitely roast the entire head with the wedges. Keep the skins on and cut it through the middle horizontally so that the cloves are exposed. They will be sticky and sweet after roasting and will taste incredible with the steak.

Preheat the oven to 400°F. Mix all the ingredients for the wedges except the garlic together in a roasting tray, then add the garlic head halves, cut-side down, and roast in the oven for 40 minutes, or until the wedges are tender, crispy and golden brown. Give them a stir halfway through.

In the meantime, make the marinade for the steak. Gently heat a small skillet and toast the cumin seeds, peppercorns and red pepper flakes together for a few minutes until they are fragrant and the seeds are golden brown. Transfer to a mortar and allow to cool for a few minutes before grinding them with a pestle. Add the turmeric and garlic and pound to a paste. Pour in the oil and add a really good pinch of salt and combine. Rub the marinade over the steaks and the sprigs of rosemary.

Heat a griddle pan or outdoor grill until very hot. Char-grill the steaks on one side for a few minutes before flipping over and cooking on the other side. Using the coated rosemary sprigs, brush extra marinade over the steaks as they cook to layer up the flavor. Cook the steaks to your liking (and it all depends on what sort you are cooking) before removing and setting aside to rest for a few minutes. This allows all the juices to run back into the meat and keep it juicy.

Serve the steaks with the spicy wedges and the sweet roasted garlic.

Prep time 15 minutes, plus
(preferably) marinating
Cook time 30 minutes

Tikka paste
2 tbsp plain Greek yogurt
1 tsp ground turmeric
1/2 tsp chile powder
1 tsp garlic paste
1 tsp ginger paste or peeled and
   finely chopped fresh ginger

6–8 boneless chicken thighs,
   skin removed and cut into
   finger-length pieces

Masala sauce
2 tbsp vegetable oil
4 green cardamom pods
1 cinnamon stick
1 tsp cumin seeds
1 large onion, finely sliced

2 tsp garlic paste
1 tsp ginger paste or peeled and
   finely chopped fresh ginger
3 fresh Indian finger chiles or
   jalapeños, 1 finely sliced and
   2 stabbed with a knife
2 tbsp garam masala
1 tbsp ground coriander
2 tsp ground cumin
1 14-oz can chopped tomatoes, or
   14 oz fresh tomatoes, chopped
1 tbsp butter (optional)
6 tbsp heavy whipping cream or
   plain Greek yogurt
good pinch of sea salt, or to taste
sugar, to taste
lemon juice, to taste
cilantro, to garnish

Chicken tikka masala

I couldn't not include a recipe for what has become the most famous Indian dish worldwide. Its story of origin varies. I was told this one:

An English army officer returning home from active duty visited his local Indian restaurant (and there weren't many around at the time). He demanded sauce with his chicken tikka, so the dutiful waiter trundled off to the kitchen to get some. The chef was fuming—tikka is always a dry dish—but to keep his customer happy he made a simple sauce from tomatoes and spices. He poured it over the chicken and, hey presto, chicken tikka masala was born!

Pouring sauce over the cooked chicken rather than allowing raw chicken to cook in the sauce is what has made this dish the most scrutinized in Indian culinary history.

Mix the tikka paste ingredients together in a bowl, add the chicken and turn to coat well. If you have time, cover and leave to marinate in the fridge overnight.

Start making the masala by gently heating the oil in a saucepan. Add the cardamom pods and cinnamon stick and wait for the cardamoms to begin turning white. Add the cumin seeds and when sizzling add the onion. Cook the onion for 5 minutes over medium-low heat so that it turns translucent and starts to color a little around the edges. Stir in the garlic, ginger and chiles. While you leave them to soften for a minute, mix the garam masala, ground coriander and cumin with a few tablespoons of water. Add to the pan and stir well. After a minute, stir through the tomatoes and butter (if using). Pour in 1 scant cup of water and leave the masala to simmer for about 15 minutes.

In the meantime, heat a griddle pan over medium heat, or preheat a grill pan or outdoor grill to medium, and cook the chicken tikka for about 10 minutes, turning often, or until cooked through.

Finish the masala sauce by stirring in the cream or yogurt (to make it lighter). Taste and adjust the flavors with salt, sugar and lemon juice if you need to.

You can either add the chicken tikka to the sauce or pour the sauce over the chicken for a truly authentic chicken tikka masala. Don't forget to scatter over fresh cilantro right at the end.

SERVES 6 TO 8
Prep time 10 minutes
Cook time about 4$^1/_2$ hours,
plus resting

1 tbsp sea salt
1 tbsp fennel seeds
1 boneless pork shoulder,
   3$^1/_2$–4$^1/_2$ lb, fat scored—your
   butcher can do this for you
2 onions, sliced
2 cinnamon sticks
2 Indian bay leaves
1 fresh red chile, sliced
2$^1/_4$ cups orange juice
$^1/_3$–$^1/_2$ cup pomegranate
   molasses

$^1/_4$ cup tamarind paste
$^1/_4$ cup white wine vinegar
2 tbsp honey
2 tbsp peeled and finely chopped
   fresh ginger
1 tbsp chipotle paste or canned
   chopped chipotle chiles
   (use less if you don't like it fiery)
2 tsp Creole mustard
good pinch of sea salt
seeds of 1 pomegranate

Slow-cooked tamarind-glazed pork

Slow cooking is one of the surest ways to seal in moisture and keep meat succulent and tender. This recipe of pork shoulder cooked low and slow, glazed with sweetly sour tamarind and pomegranate molasses, is certain to impress. There is enough fat in this cut of meat to keep the pork juicy, but I like to baste the meat often to really layer up those deeply intense flavors. Once the crackling is crispy, turn down the oven and cook the pork slowly until it falls apart.

Preheat the oven to 475°F.

Grind the salt and fennel seeds together with a pestle and mortar. Rub it all over the pork, making sure you really get it into the cuts. Lay the onions, cinnamon sticks, bay leaves and chile in the base of a roasting tray (one that fits the pork snugly) and place the pork on top, skin-side up. Pop in the oven for about 30 minutes, or until the crackling is golden brown and hard to the touch.

In the meantime, mix all the remaining ingredients except the pomegranate seeds together.

Once the crackling is ready, reduce the oven to 275°F and pour the orange juice mixture over the onions. Baste a little onto the flesh of the pork (not the crackling, or it will burn) and cook, uncovered, for about 4 hours, basting the meat every now and again. If you want to cook it longer, lower the heat. I suggest you add an extra hour of cooking time for every 25°F lower you go. The longer you cook it, the better it will be.

Take the pork out of the oven and baste one more time, including the crackling this time, then cover loosely with foil and leave to rest for around 20 minutes. The sauce in the roasting tray is going to be the gravy, so make sure you skim off any fat that rises to the top. If you prefer, you can pour the sauce into a saucepan and heat over medium heat until thickened. Discard the bay leaves.

Sprinkle the pomegranate seeds over the pork and serve with lots of the gravy and the usual trimmings of roasted potatoes and greens.

· MY SECRET ·
For perfect crackling—
and let's be honest, that's
the best bit—use paper
towels to dry off the skin so
that it is bone dry before you
rub the salt and fennel mix
deep into the cuts.

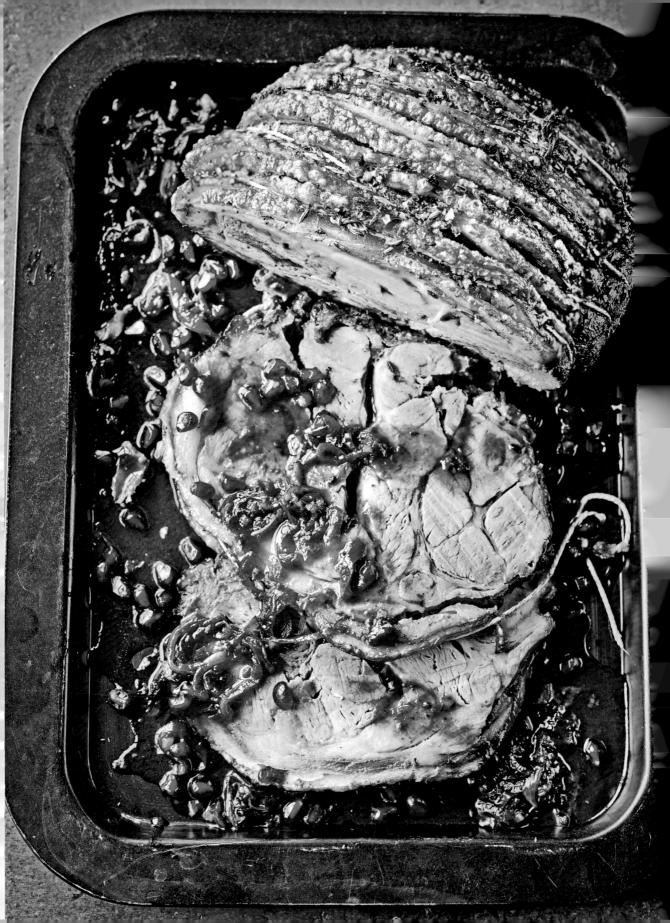

SERVES 4
Prep time 10 minutes
Cook time 45 minutes,
plus resting

1 12-oz can beer
1 tbsp peeled and roughly chopped
   fresh ginger
grated zest of 1 lime, fruit halved
   for squeezing over
1 tsp coriander seeds
1 tsp cumin seeds
3 scallions, roughly chopped
3 garlic cloves, roughly
   chopped

1 fresh red chile, roughly
   chopped
a few rosemary sprigs
1 tsp smoked paprika
1 tsp ground turmeric
2 tbsp vegetable oil—I like rapeseed
sea salt and pepper
3¼–3½ lb chicken, spatchcocked,
   legs slashed
   with a knife

Drunken chicken

The chicken isn't drunk, it's just the way you cook it! Cooking the bird over liquid—I'm using beer— keeps the meat moist and adds a little extra flavor. I've added spices to both the beer and the rub for the chicken. That way the chicken is subtly flavored inside and out and it's absolutely delicious. Try to get good-quality meat as it makes all the difference here. If you spatchcock your chicken you cut the cooking time in half. It's easy to do yourself, but you can always ask your butcher to do this for you.

Preheat the oven to 400°F.

Pour the can of beer in a deep roasting tray and add the ginger, lime zest and coriander seeds.

Make the rub for the bird. Using a food processor or pestle and mortar, grind up the cumin seeds before adding the scallions, garlic, chile and rosemary. Pulse or grind before stirring in the smoked paprika, turmeric, oil and a really good pinch of salt and pepper. Mix well to form a paste and rub it all over the chicken, inside and out. There's no harm rubbing some under the skin, too.

Lay the chicken cut-side down on a rack that will fit over the roasting tray awash with beer. Place the rack over the tray and cook in the oven for 40 minutes (or longer if your chicken is larger) and until the juices run clear. Turn the oven to broil, or transfer to a grill pan or outdoor grill preheated to medium. Allow the skin to crisp up for 5 minutes. Rest the chicken for 10 minutes before serving with a squeeze of lime and a crisp salad, such as Mixed Herb Salad with Honey Pecan Dressing (*see* page 78).

· MY SECRET ·
Why not experiment
with different beers,
such as alcoholic ginger
beer or root beer, to add
some extra flavor?

SERVES 4
Prep time 10 minutes
Cook time 10 minutes

2 tbsp vegetable oil
2 tsp black mustard seeds
1/2 tsp black peppercorns, finely crushed with a pestle and mortar
1 cinnamon stick
15–20 fresh curry leaves (*see* My Secret, page 20)—just leave them out if you don't have fresh
1 tbsp peeled and julienned fresh ginger
2 tsp garlic paste, or pound 3 garlic cloves with a pestle and mortar

3 fresh Indian finger chiles or jalapeños, 1 sliced and 2 slit down the middle but left whole
1/2 tsp ground turmeric
1 tbsp tomato paste, mixed with 2 tbsp water
1 1/4–1 1/2 lb beef fillet, cut into strips around 1/2 inch thick
good pinch of sea salt, or to taste
good pinch of sugar, or to taste
finely sliced scallions, to garnish

Chile beef with black pepper

I first tasted an Indian dish that was laced with chiles when I was on a culinary trip around coastal India a few years ago. It was pretty fiery, but underneath all that heat was a wonderful warmth and flavor. This is quite hot, so go easy on the chiles if you can't handle yours. I'm using the delicious, tender cut of beef filet, but you can use any cut you like; just make sure it's lean, otherwise it will be chewy. It's pretty quick, like a stir-fry, so try to use a wok if you have one but if not a large, heavy-bottomed skillet will do. This is a great recipe when you fancy something big on flavor but small on prep time.

Gently heat the oil in a wok, or large heavy-bottomed skillet, and add the mustard seeds, crushed peppercorns and cinnamon stick. After a minute or so the mustard seeds will be jumping out of the pan, so add the curry leaves, ginger, garlic, chiles and turmeric. Allow to soften for a minute before pouring in the tomato paste mix.

Stir well, then turn up the heat and add the beef. Keep moving it around the pan so that it colors and then turns golden brown. It will have more flavor if you allow it to caramelize, but be careful not to burn the other ingredients. The beef won't take long to cook—around a minute if you like it pink in the middle.

Taste and adjust the seasoning with salt and sugar. Sprinkle over some sliced scallions and serve with my simple Foolproof Pilau Rice (*see* page 148) and a well-needed cooling Cucumber Raita (*see* page 166).

· MY SECRET ·
Adding whole chiles, as well as sliced, gives the dish background warmth instead of burning heat. Pick them out and bite into them if you fancy a real heat kick!

SERVES 4
Prep time 20 minutes
Cook time 1 hour

Chicken
3 tbsp vegetable oil
2 large onions, finely sliced
2 tsp coriander seeds, roughly
    crushed with a pestle and mortar
1 tbsp peeled and finely chopped
    fresh ginger
2 garlic cloves, finely chopped
1 fresh red chile, Indian finger chile,
    or jalapeño, finely chopped
8 chicken joints, cut in half
    (see My Secret, opposite)—I like
    a mix of drumsticks and thighs
1½ tbsp garam masala
1 tbsp ground cumin
1 tsp ground turmeric
½ tsp chile powder (optional)
good pinch of sea salt, or to taste
6 tbsp plain Greek yogurt

Rice
1½ cups white basmati rice
6 cloves
4 green cardamom pods
2 cinnamon sticks
2 Indian bay leaves
good pinch of saffron threads
    (optional)
good pinch of sea salt, or to taste

1 tbsp peeled and julienned
    fresh ginger, for layering
2 garlic cloves, finely chopped,
    for layering
1 fresh red chile, finely chopped,
    for layering (optional)
3 tbsp roughly chopped cilantro

Chicken biryani

I always get asked what my last supper would be and this is high on my list. My partner grew up with some of the best biryanis in the world, as his family hail from Hyderabad, so I made sure I stepped up my game when I started cooking for him. This is one of his favorite meals and I hope it will become one of yours.

This is a layered biryani, which means that you cook the chicken separately and then layer it with fragrant cooked rice. I don't usually like recipes that have an ingredients list as long as your arm, but sadly this one is quite long. Trust me, it's totally worth it!

Preheat the oven to 400°F.

First, start the chicken. Gently heat half the oil in a large saucepan and cook the onions for around 10 minutes until they are light golden brown and catching around the edges. Take half out and set aside, keeping the other half frying until they are crispy—these are for layering. Take these crispy onions out and set aside for later.

Pour the remaining oil into the pan and return the first set of soft golden brown onions with the coriander seeds. Once they are sizzling, add the ginger, garlic and fresh chile. Cook for a further minute before adding the chicken, garam masala, cumin, turmeric, chile powder (if using) and enough water to come three quarters of the way up the chicken (about 1½ cups should be fine). Add a good pinch of salt, cover and leave the chicken to cook for 20 minutes.

In the meantime, get the rice ready. Rinse it in several changes of water and leave to soak in cold water for around 30 minutes. This will soften the grains so that they cook more quickly, and also will allow the beautiful flavor and fragrance to be released.

Drain the water off the rice. Fill a small saucepan with boiling water and stir in the cloves, cardamom pods, cinnamon sticks, bay leaves and saffron (if using). Add a good pinch of salt, stir and add the rice. Allow to cook uncovered for about 7 minutes, or until the grains are almost cooked through. Drain off the excess water and set aside while you finish the chicken.

Remove the chicken from the sauce and set aside. Turn off the heat and stir the yogurt into the sauce, which will thicken it. Now it's time to layer up the biryani.

In an ovenproof dish (I like to use a glass one so that you can see all the layers), start with a layer of rice. Then add some chicken and cover with a little thickened sauce. Sprinkle over some ginger, garlic and chile, followed by some of the reserved crispy onions and fresh cilantro. Keep layering up the biryani, finishing with a final layer of rice sprinkled with the last of the crispy onions and fresh cilantro, then tightly cover the dish with foil.

Pop in the oven for 15 minutes to steam and fuse the ingredients together. Serve with lots of cooling Cucumber Raita made with mint (*see* page 166) and your favorite pickles and chutneys.

· MY SECRET ·
This recipe works best if you cut the chicken legs into drumsticks and thighs, as it adds more flavor and they cook more quickly than whole joints, so ask your butcher to prepare them for you.

SERVES 4
Prep time 10 minutes
Cook time 20 minutes

2 tbsp vegetable oil, plus extra
 if needed
1 pack paneer, around 8 oz, cut into
 large bite-size pieces
20 fresh curry leaves (*see* My Secret,
 page 20) (optional)
2 tsp black mustard seeds
1 tsp cumin seeds
1 tsp ground turmeric
1 onion, finely diced
2 garlic cloves, finely chopped
1 tbsp peeled and finely chopped
 fresh ginger

2 fresh red chiles, 1 finely sliced,
 1 slit down the middle but left
 whole
2 tbsp tomato paste
1 tbsp garam masala
2 tsp ground coriander
1³/₄ cups coconut milk
4 oz (about 1³/₄ cups) broccoli florets
1 tbsp tamarind paste, or to taste
sea salt, to taste
sugar, to taste
small handful of cilantro,
 to garnish

Paneer & broccoli masala

*Making a masala from scratch
is a lot easier than you think.
I've made a few changes to a
classic recipe that uses flavors
from the shores of southern
India. Frying the paneer in
a little oil before stirring it
through the masala not
only makes it crispy but
also adds bags of flavor.*

Gently heat the oil in a saucepan and fry the paneer until it's golden brown on all sides. Remove from the pan and set aside for later.

Throw the curry leaves (if using) into the pan to crisp up. Take them out and reserve for sprinkling over at the end.

Add a little more oil to the pan if you need to and toss in the mustard and cumin seeds. Once they start sizzling, stir in the turmeric and onion. Allow to soften for a few minutes before stirring in the garlic, ginger and chiles. After a further minute, stir in the tomato paste, garam masala and coriander.

Add a splash of water to the pan and pour in the coconut milk. Bring to a simmer and toss in the broccoli and fried paneer. Stir through the tamarind and simmer for 5 minutes. Taste and adjust the seasoning with salt and sugar. Garnish with the crispy curry leaves and the fresh cilantro before serving with some steamed basmati or my Foolproof Pilau Rice (*see* page 148) to mop up the sauce.

SERVES 4 TO 6
Prep time 15 minutes
Cook time 40 minutes

1 whole skin-on salmon, about 2½ lb, cleaned, boned and head removed
1 tbsp finely chopped garlic
1 tbsp peeled and finely chopped fresh ginger
1–2 fresh red chiles, sliced
2 tbsp plain Greek yogurt
2 tsp black mustard seeds
1 tsp ground turmeric
1 tsp honey
good pinch of sea salt

8 oz crunchy vegetables—I like celery root, leeks and carrots—all julienned (about 4 cups)
20 fresh curry leaves (*see* My Secret, page 20) (optional)
1 tbsp dried unsweetened coconut, toasted (*see* My Secret, page 182) (optional)
1 tbsp roughly chopped chives
1 tbsp roughly chopped dill
2 limes, cut into quarters

Whole roasted salmon

This is my take on an ancient Indian recipe for stuffing a whole fish with spices, sealing it in an earthenware pot, burying it in the ground and covering it with natural heat fermenters. I'm using an oven to replicate the heat and I've chosen to use a whole salmon, but you can easily use individual fillets if you like. This will soon become one of your showstopper recipes that will wow all your guests.

Preheat the oven to 350°F. In the meantime, make deep cuts through the skin of the salmon.

Make the marinade for the fish by bashing together the garlic, ginger and most of the chile slices with a pestle and mortar. Mix in the yogurt, mustard seeds, turmeric, honey and a good pinch of salt. Rub the marinade all over the salmon, inside and out.

Stuff the salmon with the julienned vegetables and sprinkle in the curry leaves (if using), coconut (if using), chives and dill. Line a large roasting tray with foil and lay the fish on top. Toss in the lime quarters and roast in the oven for 40 minutes. (If using individual fillets, roast for half the time.)

Carve the fish at the table and serve with Cucumber Raita made with mint (*see* page 166) and Cumin Roast Potatoes (*see* page 146).

Pantry must-haves

As well as my spice box (see pages 37–41) there are a few ingredients I always keep stocked up. You never know when you may need them, and if I don't have time to pop to the market I know I can still eat well with my pantry must-haves.

BASMATI RICE

There are so many varieties of rice to choose from but my favorite is basmati. Grown in northern India, it has a delicate flavor and unique aroma. Some say you can smell the foothills of the Himalayas when cooking basmati and I have to agree. It's best rinsed in several changes of water to rinse off any starch, and then soaked for around half an hour to allow the grains to lengthen. This will improve the flavor of the rice and also reduce the cooking time as the grains will have softened. If you soak it for too long they will break during cooking and you will have bitty rice.

DHAL/LENTILS

Dhal/lentils last for ages and are bland, which means they carry flavor well—ideal for spice cooking. One of my favorite comfort dishes is Tadka Dhal (*see* page 154), which doesn't take long to make once the lentils are soft. With so many different varieties available you won't get bored. I like to boil more lentils than I need and pop them in the freezer. When I'm tired after a long day I just cover the frozen block in boiling water, throw in some flavors and I've got myself a fuss-free meal.

CHICKPEAS/CHANNA

You can boil them yourself but I keep the canned variety in my pantry. They taste great thrown into a salad, warmed with spices, or you can even mash them down and create a veggie burger.

CHICKPEA FLOUR/BESAN FLOUR/GRAM FLOUR

You would never make this yourself, although you could, but as it can be found at all good supermarkets you won't need to. Great for those intolerant to gluten, it has an almost nutty flavor once cooked and can be used to coat ingredients as well as thicken sauces.

CANNED TOMATOES

I think everyone should keep at least one can of chopped tomatoes in their pantry, if they don't already. Canned tomatoes are picked at their best so usually have a sweeter flavor than the store-bought tomatoes we are used to year-round. If I get great fresh tomatoes from a farmers' market I prefer to use them, otherwise I always have my canned ones to fall back on.

TOMATO PASTE

You will always find tomato paste in my pantry. I use it often, for those times I need to add a rich, intense tomato flavor to my dishes. I also like to use it as a background flavor to add warmth and sweetness to dishes, such as my Paneer & Broccoli Masala (see page 64).

TAMARIND

I prefer using the tamarind pulp (sometimes called concentrate) as all the hard work of removing the flesh from the seeds has been done for me. You can buy it in blocks that need soaking in warm water, or in a paste, which has a thick consistency and a strong concentrated flavor. You can even find whole tamarind, which look fab. Tamarind makes for fantastic chutneys (like my Sticky Sweet Date Chutney, see page 168) and adds a sweet-sour flavor to dishes such as my Slow-Cooked Tamarind-Glazed Pork (see page 54).

COCONUT MILK

I love to keep a few cans of coconut milk not only for savory recipes but also for desserts. In India people will make or buy their coconut milk fresh, which is simply done by pressing the coconut flesh. Once the liquid has settled you can separate the milk that will contain some rich coconut cream, too. Some canned brands of coconut milk contain more coconut cream than others, so I always store some cans of coconut cream in case the coconut milk's not quite thick enough.

CHAPTER 3

FEEL-GOOD FACTOR

SERVES 4
Prep time 5 minutes
Cook time 25 minutes

9 oz (about 1½ cups) quinoa, rinsed, and if necessary soaked and drained according to the packet instructions

enough vegetable stock to cook the quinoa according to the packet instructions (about 4½ cups)

1 tsp cumin seeds
1 tsp ground coriander
½ tsp ground ginger
1 large carrot, sliced into ribbons using a vegetable peeler

2 scallions, finely sliced
8 sun-dried tomatoes in oil, drained and sliced
3 tbsp roughly chopped cilantro
2 tbsp olive oil
juice of 1 lime, plus extra wedges for serving
sea salt and pepper
seeds of 1 pomegranate, to garnish (optional)
plain Greek yogurt, to serve

Quinoa with carrot & lime

Quinoa is a seed that has become one of the most sought-after ingredients to add to your diet. Loved by vegans and those with a gluten allergy, it's packed with protein, including all eight of the essential amino acids your body needs. Healthy or what?! It can be slightly bitter and therefore some varieties call for washing and soaking them first, so have a read of the packet instructions before cooking. You will have to boil it for around 20 minutes and either wait for the liquid to be absorbed or drain it off. I like to use vegetable stock instead of plain boring water, and add some spices to give it a burst of life. I read that there are around 1,800 varieties of quinoa, so use whatever color you prefer.

Cook the quinoa according to the packet instructions, using vegetable stock instead of water and stirring in the cumin seeds and ground coriander and ginger, until the stock has been absorbed and the quinoa is soft and plump.

You can either leave the quinoa to cool before mixing in the remaining ingredients (except the pomegranate seeds and yogurt) or you can toss it all together while still hot. Taste and adjust the seasoning if you need to. Sprinkle over the pomegranate seeds (if using) to garnish and serve with some yogurt and lime wedges on the side.

· MY SECRET ·
You can use couscous instead of quinoa. I like the giant type. Cook according to the packet instructions in vegetable stock, adding the spices to the boiling hot stock. You may need to add a little more seasoning, as couscous doesn't have as much flavor as quinoa.

SERVES 4
Prep time 5 minutes
Cook time around 30 minutes

1 fennel bulb, trimmed and
   thinly sliced
3 tbsp olive oil
1 tsp cumin seeds
1/4 tsp ground turmeric
4 garlic cloves, kept in their skins
3/4 lb green beans
zest (pared in large pieces) and
   juice of 1/2 lemon

2 scallions, finely sliced
1 fresh red chile, seeded if
   you don't like your salads fiery,
   finely sliced
4 cups spinach leaves
2 tbsp roughly chopped mint leaves
sea salt
1 tbsp sesame seeds, toasted, to
   sprinkle (optional)

Green bean salad with mint, roasted fennel & garlic

Fennel seed is a spice that often divides people, as it has a strong aniseed flavor. The fresh fennel bulb also has a very overpowering flavor, but when roasted it becomes sweet and mellow. I love adding spices before it's roasted to give some depth and then tossing it through greens while it's still warm for a pick-me-up salad.

Preheat the oven to 400°F. Put the fennel slices in a roasting tray and drizzle over half the oil. Rub them with the cumin seeds and turmeric and then add the garlic cloves. Roast for 25 minutes until the fennel is lightly golden brown at the edges. Remove from the oven and allow to cool a little.

In the meantime, blanch the green beans by cooking them in a saucepan of boiling water with the lemon zest. Cook for 2 minutes before draining and plunging them into ice-cold water to keep their vibrant green color. Discard the lemon zest.

Toss the green beans together with the scallions, chile, spinach and mint in a bowl.

When cool enough to handle, squeeze the roasted garlic cloves out of their skins and roughly chop them before adding them to the salad with the warm fennel. Drizzle over the remaining oil and the lemon juice, then taste and season with salt accordingly, before serving sprinkled with the toasted sesame seeds, if you wish.

Bapuji (left) and Baa (back right) with their six children (including Dad—front) at Allcroft Road, London. Baa was clearly used to cooking in large batches with all those mouths to feed!

Mum's mother, Hansa, loved to dance. She was a dentist by profession but always found time to indulge in her favorite hobby.

Mum and her brother, Ajay
Uncle to me, with Tintin (right)
and dressed up for a family
get-together (below right).

Mum's father, Naishad, was
an officer in the Indian army.
This photo was taken when he
was young but he quickly rose
through the ranks and soon
became a colonel. Growing up
traveling to and from different
army bases meant that Mum
saw a lot of India from a very
young age.

4 cups mixed salad leaves
1 large carrot, sliced into ribbons using a vegetable peeler
1 red onion, finely sliced
1³/₄ oz drained sun-dried tomatoes in oil (oil reserved— see right), roughly chopped
8 tbsp mixed herbs, roughly chopped—I like a mix of cilantro, mint, basil and parsley

2 tbsp oil—I like to use the oil from the sun-dried tomatoes but canola oil or olive oil is fine
1 tbsp honey
2 tsp mustard—spicy brown or whatever type you like
juice of 1 lemon, or to taste
good pinch of sea salt, or to taste
1³/₄ oz (about ½ cup) pecan halves, roughly chopped

Mixed herb salad with honey pecan dressing

I love salads and am always thinking of new ways to dress them up. Sometimes I try out different leaves, but usually I play around with the ingredients in my pantry to see what dressings I can make. This is a simple salad with a trusty honey pecan dressing.

Toss together the salad leaves, carrot, red onion, sun-dried tomatoes and herbs.

Make the dressing by whisking all the remaining ingredients together, adding the pecans once everything is combined. Taste and add more salt or lemon juice if you need to.

Lightly dress the salad with the dressing before piling high and tucking in.

· MY SECRET ·
For a little more crunch, drench the pecans in honey on a rimmed baking sheet and roast in a preheated oven at 350°F for 10 minutes while you prepare the other ingredients. Then toss through the salad. Simply divine.

SERVES 4
Prep time 5 minutes
Cook time up to 30 minutes

1¼ lb mixed-colored raw beets, peeled and cut into wedges
2 tbsp canola oil
1 tsp black mustard seeds
1 tsp ground ginger
1¾ oz (about ½ cup) whole blanched hazelnuts
5½ oz paneer, cut into large bite-size pieces

2 tbsp plain Greek yogurt
1 tbsp horseradish sauce
juice of ½ lemon
1 tbsp roughly chopped dill
good pinch of sea salt
drizzle of honey, to taste
2 cups watercress

Paneer & roasted beet salad

Paneer is a cow's-milk cheese that has a texture similar to haloumi. Now I know that this is a recipe to make you feel good and so should be low in fat, but I have used paneer for a little indulgence. And I figured if I'm going to have the cheese, then I might as well cook it the way it tastes best, which is to pan-fry it so that the edges go slightly crispy. But you can leave it out altogether if you like. I always eat with my eyes, so I'm using different-colored beets.

Preheat the oven to 400°F. Put the beets in a roasting tray and drizzle over half the oil. Rub them with the mustard seeds and ginger and roast for 25 minutes. Add the hazelnuts and allow them to toast with the beets for 5 minutes.

In the meantime, gently heat up the remaining oil in a skillet, add the pieces of paneer and fry, moving them around often, until they are golden brown on all sides. Drain on paper towels while you make the dressing.

Whisk together the yogurt, horseradish, lemon juice, dill, salt and honey in a small bowl.

Remove the roasted beets and toasted hazelnuts from the oven, then toss with the paneer, watercress and dressing.

SERVES 4
Prep time 5 minutes
Cook time 10–15 minutes

2 tbsp olive oil
1 tbsp tamarind paste
1 tbsp honey
1 garlic clove, crushed
1 tsp cumin seeds, toasted (*see* page 171) and roughly crushed with a pestle and mortar
good pinch of sea salt, or to taste
good pinch of cracked black peppercorns

2 large eggplants, thinly sliced crosswise
1 large red chile
1 red onion, finely sliced
7 oz drained canned chickpeas
2 cups arugula leaves
juice of 1/2 lime
2 1/4 oz feta cheese (optional)

Roast eggplant salad with chickpeas & tamarind

This is perfect to have when you fancy something good for you, but you definitely need something carby to bulk it out. Eggplants are one of the best ingredients to pair with spices, as they are like sponges and soak up any flavors you put with them. For this recipe I have made a marinade that doubles up as a dressing.

Preheat a griddle pan over a fairly high heat or, if baking in the oven, set it to 400°F.

Make the marinade/dressing by mixing together the olive oil, tamarind, honey, garlic, cumin, salt and cracked pepper.

Rub half the marinade on the eggplant slices and whole chile, add to the hot griddle pan and cook for around 10 minutes, turning a couple of times, until soft. If cooking in the oven, spread out on a rimmed baking sheet and bake for around 15 minutes, turning once.

Once the eggplant is cooked, roughly chop the chile. Toss the red onion, chickpeas and arugula with the lime juice and remaining dressing in a bowl. Gently mix in the eggplant and chopped chile. Serve piled high, with some crumbly salty feta if you fancy it.

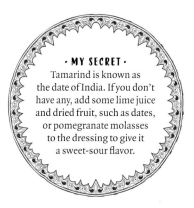

· MY SECRET ·
Tamarind is known as the date of India. If you don't have any, add some lime juice and dried fruit, such as dates, or pomegranate molasses to the dressing to give it a sweet-sour flavor.

SERVES 4
Prep time 5 minutes
Cook time 2 minutes

3 tbsp olive oil
1 tbsp coriander seeds
$1/4$ tsp black peppercorns, lightly crushed with a pestle and mortar
30 cherry tomatoes (mixed colors look great), halved or quartered depending on size, or 4 large tomatoes, thickly sliced

1 small red onion, finely sliced
good pinch of sea salt
2 tbsp basil leaves
good drizzle of balsamic vinegar
$4^1/2$ oz burrata (or mozzarella)

Tomato & red onion salad with toasted coriander & burrata

One of my favorite chefs serves a dish similar to this at his restaurant in London. I have added some more spices to mine and combined it with the traditional tomato and red onion salad that I loved growing up. Burrata is similar to mozzarella but contains cream to make it richer. It tastes divine, so do seek it out for this recipe.

Gently heat the oil in a small skillet and add the coriander seeds and peppercorns. As soon as they start sizzling, turn off the heat and allow them to scent the oil.

Delicately toss the tomatoes with the red onion in a bowl. Season with a good pinch of salt and spoon over half the toasted spices, including some of the scented oil. Toss to coat the ingredients evenly before sprinkling over the basil leaves and drizzling with balsamic vinegar.

Leaving the burrata whole, place with the salad and top with the remaining toasted spices. This is a real sharing salad, so rip open the burrata as you serve it.

SERVES 4
Prep time 20 minutes

1 shallot, finely chopped
1 tbsp peeled and finely chopped
   fresh ginger
1–2 fresh red chiles, seeded if
   you don't like your salads
   with a chile kick
1 tbsp palm sugar, or to taste,
   roughly chopped, or brown sugar
juice of 1 lime
1¹/₂ tbsp light or dark soy sauce,
   or to taste
2 tbsp toasted sesame oil

1 cucumber
15 radishes, trimmed and
   finely sliced
10¹/₂ oz mixed bean sprouts
   or mixed pea and bean sprouts
   (*see* My Secret, page 96)
3 tbsp roughly chopped mint, plus
   whole leaves to garnish (optional)
1³/₄ oz salted peanuts, roughly
   crushed

Radish, peanut & mint salad

I came across some amazing salads when I visited Thailand a few years ago to learn about Thai cooking. When I got home, the first thing I did was stock up on all those essential Thai ingredients and I've been using them in my cooking ever since. Here I've used palm sugar to give my dressing a little sweetness, but you can use brown sugar if you don't have any.

Make the dressing by pounding the shallot, ginger and chiles with a pestle and mortar. Add the palm sugar and pound again until it's all dissolved. Stir in the lime juice, soy sauce and sesame oil. Taste and add more soy sauce if you prefer it saltier, and palm sugar for extra sweetness.

Slice the cucumber into thin ribbons using a knife or a vegetable peeler. Make sure you use the skin too, as this will add a lovely color and flavor to the salad. Stop when you reach the watery core. Mix the cucumber ribbons with the radishes, sprouts and most of both the mint and peanuts in a bowl.

Pour in the dressing and toss well to coat. Serve sprinkled with the remaining mint and peanuts for the ultimate crunchy Asian salad.

· MY SECRET ·
This salad tastes best when dressed just before you serve it. You can make the dressing beforehand and toss it through the crunchy salad at the last minute.

Magical chiles

Chiles are truly incredible. They come in all sorts of shapes and sizes and their heat levels vary considerably from pleasantly warm through to eye-wateringly hot. They are full of antioxidants, high in vitamin C that will help keep that cold at bay, and can help reduce cholesterol—they really are magical. When I was young you could buy only one type of mild chile from the supermarket, and the fiery Indian finger chiles were only available from the Indian shop. Now you can buy all sorts of exotic varieties, each with its own unique flavor.

Each and every one of us has a different chile tolerance and each chile you buy or grow will never be the same as the last, which is why I always test every chile before I add it to a recipe. Some people like to follow recipes exactly to the letter, and never improvise with the ingredient list. When cooking with spice and heat I think it's essential to change the recipe slightly.

If a recipe says three chiles, should you throw in three? Your chiles may be very different from the ones used by the chef who created it or—worst of all—yours may be much hotter. Of course you can always snip the end off a chile and have a nibble to check the heat, but it's pretty risky as it could blow your head off! I find it better to snip the end and then have a little smell. If it burns your nose, then it's likely to burn everything else. If

you can't sense any heat, simply rub the cut end with your fingertip and tap the inside of your lip.

The general rule of thumb is the larger the chile, the milder it is, but I have been caught out one too many times using this guide alone. It really is worth checking every chile: you'll always get that one rogue that is either crazy hot or has no heat whatsoever.

The seeds and the white membrane inside the chile carry most of the heat, which can easily be removed if you want to tone down a recipe. If doing this, save the seeds and dry them out. You can sow them and have a flourishing chile plant in no time. Be patient: the white flowers bloom before you see any green chiles. You can pick them green and use them fresh or freeze them, or leave them on the plant to change to yellow, orange, red and sometimes even purple (only in very hot climates). Chiles taste sweeter as they ripen and the red ones dry the best. The ultimate question is which are hotter—green or red? If they are the same variety then they will be the same in heat, but ripe red chiles are sweeter than the underripe green ones.

If you want to add some extra flavor to your dishes as well as heat then try some of these chile varieties:

JALAPEÑOS
They are around 3 inches long and usually eaten when green. They have a mild citrus flavor and are quite fiery.

CHIPOTLE
This is one of my favorite chiles. It's a smoked, dried jalapeño, which carries the same heat as a standard jalapeño but is slightly sweeter and has a beautiful smoky flavor. Try with Spicy Smoky Potatoes (see page 106).

FINGER CHILES
There are different types of finger chiles but I'm talking about the Indian ones. They are thin and as long as your finger (hence the name), and pretty hot even for my standards. They are usually sold green, but if you grow your own you should try them when red, as they are delicious. Finger chiles are used in Chile Beef with Black Pepper and in Black Dahl (see pages 60 and 140).

HABANERO
This is a really hot variety and is usually used in Mexican cooking. You will see them when they are orange or red so buy what you can find and only use a little bit; I tend to use one to serve four people. The habanero has a tropical flavor and goes great in tomato dishes.

SCOTCH BONNET
One of the fieriest chiles around, Scotch bonnets are very VERY hot and they originate from the Caribbean. They are also known as Ball of Fire because that's exactly what they are! Once you get past the heat you will see they have a fruity flavor that is rather nice.

CHAPTER
4
VEGGIES GALORE

SERVES 4
Prep time 10 minutes
Cook time 1 hour

2 butternut squash, cut in half
    lengthwise and seeds removed
1 tsp cumin seeds
1/2 tsp coriander seeds
1/2 tsp black peppercorns
1/2 tsp crushed red pepper flakes
1 tsp garam masala
1 tbsp vegetable oil or light olive oil

1 cup spinach leaves, roughly
    chopped
1 3/4 oz feta cheese, crumbled
2 garlic cloves, finely chopped
2 tbsp finely chopped mint leaves
6 sun-dried tomatoes in oil, drained
    and roughly chopped
grated zest and juice of 1 lemon

Balti-baked squash with feta, tomato & mint

Baked butternut squash rubbed with balti spices and filled with salty feta, sweet sun-dried tomatoes and fresh mint. No wonder this is a great veggie dish that is filling and packs a lot of flavor.

There is no recipe as such for "balti," as it actually refers to the pot that the dish is cooked in rather than a particular spice mix. However, across the world you can find balti spice blends and they typically contain the spices I have used in this recipe, so I have called this dish a balti in terms of the particular spicing of the dish.

Preheat the oven 400°F. Lay the squash, cut-side up, on a rimmed baking sheet.

Roughly crush the cumin and coriander seeds, peppercorns and red pepper flakes with a pestle and mortar before mixing in the garam masala and oil. Rub all over the squash, especially on the flesh side, and bake in the oven for 45 minutes, or until you can put a knife through the flesh of the squash easily.

In the meantime, make the filling by mixing together the spinach, feta, garlic, mint, sun-dried tomatoes and lemon juice.

When the squash is soft, take out of the oven and scoop out nearly all the flesh, leaving a 1/2-inch border of flesh around the inside of each squash half. Mix the scooped-out squash with the filling and pop it all back into the grooves you have just carved out. Sprinkle over the lemon zest and roast in the oven for a further 10 minutes. Serve with a delicious crisp salad, such as Green Bean Salad with Mint, Roasted Fennel & Garlic (*see* page 74).

SERVES 4 AS A SIDE
Prep time 10 minutes,
plus soaking
Cook time 15 minutes

2 cans drained chickpeas
6 tea bags—any variety of
   English Breakfast tea will do
2 tbsp vegetable oil
2 scallions, finely sliced
4 cloves
4 green cardamom pods
2 tsp cumin seeds
1/2 tsp ground turmeric
2 garlic cloves, finely chopped
1 tbsp peeled and finely chopped
   fresh ginger

3–4 fresh Indian finger chiles or
   jalapeño, slit down the middle
   but left whole
1 tsp coriander seeds
8 cherry tomatoes, cut in half
sea salt, to taste
sugar, to taste
juice of 1/2 lemon, or to taste
cilantro, to garnish
plain Greek yogurt, to serve

Chai chickpeas

An old recipe I came across when I was learning about food eaten by the royal Moghul emperors provided the inspiration for this dish. Uncooked chickpeas are soaked overnight with tea leaves so that the deep, earthy flavor of the tea permeates all the way through them. I love this idea, as there are so many chickpea dishes out there that are pretty boring and tasteless. This one has real depth, but I don't imagine you will want to soak dried chickpeas overnight and then wait 30 minutes for them to boil the next day. So I'm using ready-cooked canned chickpeas to reduce the cooking time and soaking them in water with tea bags. If you don't have time to soak the chickpeas overnight and want to make the dish right away, then just brew an extra-strong cup of tea and add that as your tea liquor.

Soak the chickpeas with the tea bags in a bowl of cold water overnight. The next day, drain the chickpeas through a sieve, discarding the tea bags but saving the tea liquor.

Gently heat a skillet with the oil and add the scallions, cloves and cardamoms. After a minute, stir in half the cumin seeds and the turmeric, garlic, ginger and chiles. Allow to soften for a minute while you finely crush the remaining cumin seeds and the coriander seeds with a pestle and mortar. Add these to the pan with a good splash of the tea liquor and allow the spices to release their essential oils for a minute or two.

Stir through the tomatoes, add the chickpeas and season with salt and a good pinch of sugar, then pour in enough tea liquor to cover the chickpeas. Leave to cook for 10 minutes before tasting and adjusting the seasoning if you think it needs it. The lemon juice will pep it up, so squeeze in a little if you aren't sure how much it needs.

Serve garnished with the cilantro, along with a good dollop of the yogurt.

SERVES 4 AS A SIDE
Prep time 10 minutes
Cook time 15 minutes

2 large eggplants
2 tbsp vegetable oil
2 tsp black mustard seeds
1 scallion, finely sliced
1 fresh red chile, sliced
2 garlic cloves, finely sliced
good drizzle of honey
1 tsp ground cumin

good pinch of sea salt, or to taste
juice of $1/2$ lemon or lime, or to taste
cilantro, to garnish

Smoked eggplant masala

Otherwise known as bhaingan bharta, this is a recipe for an ingredient I once hated. Eggplants have a tendency to go quite slimy once cooked, but only if they are allowed to stew in liquid, which is why I never used to like them. This recipe will change your perception of them forever. They are gently smoked—so try this on the outdoor grill—and then mixed with all sorts of tasty treats. A traditional bhaingan bharta is slightly different from my version.

Score the eggplants around the top by the stalk and again down to the base, as if you are trying to mark where you would cut it into quarters. This will help the skin come off once the eggplants are smoked. Place them on a wire rack over a medium flame on a gas burner to allow the skin to char (or place directly on the rack of an outdoor grill over medium heat). Keep moving them around so that all the skin turns coal black and starts to flake. This should take about 5 minutes.

Using tongs or an oven glove, transfer the eggplants to a bowl and cover with plastic wrap while you prepare the other ingredients. This will give the eggplants time to cool down enough so that you can peel them.

Carefully peel the eggplants and discard the blackened skin. Mash the flesh with a fork.

Gently heat the oil in a large skillet and add the mustard seeds. Cook for a minute until they start jumping out of the pan, then stir in the scallion, chile and garlic. Allow to cook for another minute before stirring in the smoky eggplant flesh. Drizzle over the honey and stir in the cumin with a good pinch of salt. Stir and leave to cook for a few minutes before squeezing in some lemon or lime juice and tasting. Adjust the seasoning if you need to and serve garnished with some fresh cilantro.

· MY SECRET ·
You can char the skin of the eggplants on a hot grill or under a broiler. Just make sure you turn them often so that all the skin gets colored and smoky.

SERVES 4
Prep time 10 minutes

1 red onion, finely sliced
1 tbsp white wine vinegar
4 cups sprouted lentils, or
  other mixed bean sprouts or
  mixed pea and bean sprouts
  (*see* My Secret, below)
4 cups spinach leaves
1 fresh red chile, seeds removed
  and finely sliced
8 cherry tomatoes, cut in half
2 tbsp roughly chopped cilantro

1 tbsp roughly chopped
  mint leaves
seeds of 1 pomegranate
2 tbsp olive oil
1 tsp spicy brown mustard
1 tsp cumin seeds, toasted
  (*see* page 171)
1 tsp honey
juice of 1 lemon or lime
good pinch of sea salt and pepper

Lentil salad with toasted cumin dressing

This salad is packed with goodness, with its sprouted lentils mixed with red onions, spinach and pomegranate seeds, and all tossed with a toasted cumin dressing. I'm using green lentils (green mung beans), which are easy to sprout yourself, but it does take some time. If you would rather save yourself the hassle, then just buy a pack of mixed bean sprouts, or mixed pea and bean sprouts, instead.

Mix the red onion and white wine vinegar together in a glass or ceramic bowl. Set aside while you prepare the other ingredients. The onions will start to release their color and turn beautifully pink.

Toss the sprouted lentils with the spinach, chile, tomatoes, cilantro, mint and pomegranate seeds in a large bowl. Add the onions and mix well.

Make the dressing by whisking the remaining ingredients together. Pour over the salad, toss to combine and serve piled high for a great meal packed with superfoods.

· MY SECRET ·
Sprouting lentils is easy but it takes time. Rinse them thoroughly and leave to soak overnight. Drain, rinse and leave to sprout in a colander, covered with a clean, dark tea towel. Rinse and drain them every morning and night, moving them around to sprout evenly, until they are as sprouted as you like them.

SERVES 4
Prep time 20 minutes
Cook time 15 minutes

olive oil, for greasing and drizzling
9 oz ricotta cheese
1 fresh red chile, seeds removed if
    you don't want it fiery (optional)
grated zest and juice of $1/2$ lemon
1 scallion, finely sliced
2 garlic cloves, finely chopped
1 tbsp roughly chopped chives,
    plus extra to garnish
good pinch of sea salt and pepper

1 small naan bread, about $1^3/_4$ oz
1 tbsp freshly grated Parmesan
    cheese
1 tbsp mixed unsalted nuts
    (optional)
4 peppers, preferably Romano, cut
    in half lengthwise and seeded
aged balsamic vinegar, for drizzling
    (optional)

Stuffed sweet peppers

I think we've all had our fair share of bad stuffed peppers. Usually, they are loaded with rice and veg and baked until soft and often lifeless. This version doesn't have a grain of rice in sight and instead uses creamy ricotta to add a little indulgence. I've also topped them with some bread crumbs made from leftover naan bread, but just use whatever bread you have—a little stale is good! The best peppers for this are the long, sweet Romano ones, but regular bell peppers will do.

Preheat the oven to 425°F and grease a rimmed baking sheet with a little oil.

Make the stuffing for the peppers by mixing together the ricotta, chile (if using), lemon juice, scallion, garlic, chives and salt and pepper in a bowl.

Make the topping by blitzing the naan bread, Parmesan, mixed nuts (if using) and lemon zest together in a food processor until finely ground.

Fill the peppers generously with the ricotta mixture and sprinkle over the bread-crumb mix. Set on the baking sheet and bake in the oven for 15 minutes. You may need to loosely cover them with foil if the bread crumbs start to color too much.

Remove from the oven, garnish with the chives and drizzle with olive oil and balsamic vinegar if you like. This is a stuffed pepper you will be proud of.

SERVES 4
Prep time 10 minutes
Cook time 1 1/4 hours

3 fresh red chiles, 2 for roasting whole and 1, thinly sliced, to garnish
3 tbsp oil—I like canola oil or light olive oil
2 onions, finely sliced
2 Indian bay leaves
1 tsp cumin seeds
1 tbsp garam masala
3 carrots, diced
2 celery sticks, diced
2 garlic cloves, finely chopped

10 1/2 oz dried lentils—I like green or brown lentils—rinsed, soaked in water for 30 minutes, then drained
6 1/2 cups hot vegetable stock
3 1/2 oz broccoli florets or baby broccoli (about 2 cups)
2 handfuls of spinach leaves
juice of 1/2 lemon, or to taste
sea salt and pepper
4 tbsp low-fat plain Greek yogurt, to garnish

Spiced vegetable soup with lentils & roasted chile

Soups are the ultimate comfort food. I've made this dish hundreds of times and it never fails to hit the spot. You can use any vegetables you like, but I'm going for carrots, broccoli and spinach, and I'm using lentils to add some body to it. As I love chiles I'm adding them in two different ways, roasted and then fresh; but you don't need to roast them if you don't want to.

Start by roasting the chiles. If you have a gas stove, place a wire rack over an open flame and roast your chiles on top until they are blistered and black. If not, use a broiler or outdoor grill, making sure it is really hot. Keep turning the chiles so that they color evenly, about 5 minutes. Transfer to a bowl, cover with plastic wrap and let cool.

While the chiles are roasting and cooling, start the soup. Gently heat 2 tablespoons of the oil in a large saucepan and fry the onions for about 10 minutes until they have turned light golden brown. Take half out and set aside. Cook the onions in the pan for a further 5 minutes, or until they are deep golden brown and crispy. These are for sprinkling over at the end. Take these out of the pan and reserve.

Pour the remaining tablespoon of oil into the pan and add the bay leaves and cumin seeds. Put the softened onions back in (that's the first set you took out of the pan) and add the garam masala, carrots, celery, garlic and lentils. Carefully peel the charred skin off the chiles, roughly chop (with or without seeds, it's up to you) and add to the pan. Stir well and leave to cook for 5 minutes before pouring in the hot stock. Bring the soup to a simmer and allow to cook for 40 minutes, or until the carrots and lentils have softened.

Remove from the heat, discard the bay leaves, and blitz the soup a few times using an immersion blender. I like to leave some texture in there. Put back on the heat and stir in the broccoli. After 2 minutes, stir in the spinach and turn off the heat. Taste the soup and add salt, pepper, and lemon juice to taste. Serve topped with a cooling dollop of yogurt, the reserved crispy onions and the sliced chile.

SERVES 4
Prep time 15 minutes,
plus (preferably) chilling
Cook time around 8 minutes

2 tbsp vegetable oil
2 tsp cumin seeds
3 scallions, finely sliced
2 garlic cloves, finely chopped
1 fresh red chile, finely chopped
1 tsp smoked paprika
1 14-oz can mixed beans, drained
    and roughly mashed

2 tbsp roughly chopped
    cilantro
2 tbsp roughly chopped chives
good pinch of sea salt and pepper
4 burger buns, to serve

Spicy bean burgers

Most meat lovers would never pick a bean burger, but this is a great recipe packed with flavor for those meat-free days. Make sure you use ready-cooked canned mixed beans, as it saves so much time and effort in soaking dried beans and then boiling them up. And remember that beans are quite bland, so I've been bold with my flavors and spices.

Gently heat half the oil in a small skillet and add the cumin seeds. When they start to sizzle, stir in the scallions, garlic and chile, and allow to fry for 30 seconds before sprinkling in the smoked paprika. Add a splash of water to stop it from burning. When all the water has evaporated, pour the mixture into the mashed beans in a bowl. Add the cilantro, chives and salt and pepper, and mix well.

Form the bean mixture into burger shapes. Lay on a plate, cover and pop in the fridge for 30 minutes to firm up, if you have time.

When you are ready to cook, gently heat the remaining oil in a skillet and fry the chilled burgers for a few minutes on each side, only turning them over when they are golden brown. Serve in a burger bun, along with all your favorite trimmings.

I like to make large batches of these burgers and freeze some for another day. Just lay the uncooked burgers on a baking sheet and pop in the freezer instead of the fridge. Once the burgers are firm, you can then pack them together in a freezer container or bag and freeze until you need them. To cook from frozen, preheat the oven to 350°F, place the burgers on a baking sheet and cook for 30 to 35 minutes, or until cooked through.

SERVES 4 AS A SNACK
Prep time 10 minutes,
plus cooling
Cook time 30 minutes

1 lb potatoes, cut into small pieces
1/2 tsp ground turmeric
zest, pared in large pieces,
 and juice of 1 lemon
sea salt
3 tbsp vegetable oil
1 tsp black mustard seeds
3 fat garlic cloves, finely chopped

1 tsp peeled and finely chopped
 fresh ginger
really good pinch of chile powder
2 tbsp finely chopped cilantro
3 1/2 oz fresh or frozen peas, run
 under boiling water
3 tbsp semolina

Aloo tikkis

This is a recipe for traditional Indian potato cakes—mashed potatoes delicately spiced and filled with peas and then pan-fried until golden and crispy. They are often served with chutneys, so rummage through the pantry and get some of your favorites out. I prefer to stuff the mash with peas, but you can stir them through if you like. It's worth rolling them in semolina to get them really crispy, but they still taste great without.

Fill a saucepan with cold water, add the potatoes with the turmeric, a few large pieces of lemon zest and a good pinch of salt and bring to a boil. Cook for about 15 minutes, or until the potatoes are soft.

Drain the potatoes and leave to steam and dry out in the colander while you temper the spices and the holy trinity of garlic, ginger and chile. Gently heat 1 tablespoon of the oil in a skillet and add the mustard seeds. When they start to jump out of the pan, stir through the garlic, ginger and chile powder.

Transfer the potatoes to a bowl and pour the tempered spices over the top. Add a good pinch of salt, squeeze over the lemon juice and stir in the cilantro. Taste and add more chile powder if you like it fiery.

Using a fork, mash the potatoes and spread them out so that they cool quickly. When they are cool enough to handle, start making the tikkis by putting about a tablespoonful of mash in your hand and flattening it out. Get about a teaspoonful of the blanched peas and put them in the center. Wrap the mashed potatoes around them as if the peas were a stuffing. Flatten it slightly, making sure the peas don't push their way through. Continue to make tikkis until you have used up all the mash and peas.

Preheat the oven to 200°F. Gently heat the remaining oil in a large skillet. Roll the tikkis in the semolina and fry, in batches, on all sides until golden and crispy. Keep the cooked ones warm in the oven while you fry the rest. Serve with your favorite chutney such as tomato chutney (*see page 32*).

· MY SECRET ·
I like to pop my tikkis in the fridge for about 30 minutes after I've formed them, to give them time to firm up so that they hold their shape better after frying.

SERVES 4 AS A SIDE
Prep time 5 minutes
Cook time 45 minutes

1¼ lb potatoes (any sort will do), skins left on and scrubbed
1 tsp ground turmeric
1 dried chipotle chile or 1 tsp chipotle paste or canned chopped chipotle chiles (use less if you don't like it fiery)
1 tbsp white urad dhal (split and skinned lentils) (optional)
2 tsp fenugreek seeds (see My Secret, below)
2 tbsp vegetable oil or light olive oil
2 tsp black mustard seeds

2 tsp cumin seeds
1 tsp smoked paprika
3 garlic cloves, finely sliced
3 scallions, finely sliced
pinch of sea salt, or to taste
juice of 1 lime, plus extra lime halves for squeezing over

To garnish
2 tbsp chopped cilantro
2 heaped tbsp salted peanuts, roughly chopped

Spicy smoky potatoes

I first tasted potatoes like this at one of my favorite restaurants when I moved to London. They were divine—charred in all the right places with a hint of smokiness and suitably spicy. They had a strange crunch to them that I soon figured out was fried lentils (in this case white urad dhal), so I have added these and a little more crunch right at the end in the form of peanuts, but if you don't fancy them, just leave them out.

Fill a saucepan with cold water, add the potatoes with the turmeric and chipotle chile and bring to a boil, then cook until soft. Depending on how large the potatoes are, this could take up to 30 minutes. Drain them once they are soft, reserving the boiled softened chipotle chile if you used one.

Gently heat a heavy-bottomed skillet and toast the urad dhal (if using) and fenugreek seeds until nutty and fragrant and starting to turn golden brown. Pour over the oil and add the mustard and cumin seeds. Once they start to sizzle, add the smoked paprika, garlic and scallions, and allow them to soften for a minute or so. Finely chop the reserved chipotle chile (if you used one) and stir this through. Add the potatoes and use a fork to break them up slightly.

Season with a little salt, remembering you are going to sprinkle over some salted peanuts later, and squeeze over the lime juice. Taste and adjust the seasoning. To make this dish extra crunchy, leave the potatoes to cook and slightly catch on the base of the pan. Stir them every now and again until crispy and golden brown all over.

Serve sprinkled with the cilantro and salted nuts, with lime halves to squeeze over, for an ultimate veggie side dish.

· MY SECRET ·
Fenugreek seeds, also known as methi seeds, are unusually bitter and incredibly hard, but once cooked they soften and add a nutty flavor to dishes. Sprouted methi leaves are milder and are a great substitute for spinach.

SERVES 4
Prep time 15 minutes
Cook time 5 minutes per
batch of fritters

Fritters
3/4 cup gram (chickpea) flour
1 tsp baking powder
1 tsp smoked paprika
1 tsp cumin seeds
good pinch of sea salt and pepper
2 eggs, beaten
1/4 cup plus 1 tbsp milk
7 oz corn, drained if canned
    or defrosted if frozen
2 scallions, finely sliced
2 garlic cloves, finely chopped
1–2 fresh red chiles, finely sliced
1 tbsp roughly chopped chives
2 tbsp vegetable oil, plus extra
    as needed

Avocado salsa
1 avocado, peeled, pitted and
    roughly chopped
1 red onion, finely chopped
6 cherry tomatoes or 1 large
    tomato, finely chopped
1 tbsp roughly chopped mint
good pinch of sea salt, or to taste
good drizzle of honey
juice of 1 lime, or to taste

Corn fritters with avocado salsa

I'm not a big fan of the word fritter, but I can't think of another name for these. They are like veggie-packed savory pancakes, and if you have time to make the salsa I highly recommend it. I have used gram (chickpea) flour, which is gluten free, but you can use all-purpose flour if you don't have any.

This recipe is like a ray of sunshine—so refreshing and light. It's great to have for brunch or a healthy snack.

Make the batter for the fritters by mixing together the flour, baking powder, smoked paprika, cumin seeds and salt and pepper in a bowl. In another bowl, whisk together the eggs and milk before pouring it into the dry mix. Beat together well until smooth and leave to stand while you prepare the rest of the ingredients.

Mix the corn, scallions, garlic, chile and chives together in a separate bowl. Add enough of the batter to coat them well—they should be a dropping consistency.

Preheat the oven to 200°F. Heat a skillet with the oil, then add around 2 tablespoonfuls of the batter per fritter to the hot oil and cook for about 3 minutes until light golden brown on the underside before flipping over and cooking the other side for a couple of minutes. Keep the cooked fritters warm in the oven while you fry the rest, adding more oil to coat the base of the pan if you need to.

In the meantime, make the salsa by mixing all the ingredients together in a serving bowl, tasting and adjusting the flavorings as necessary. Serve with the warm fritters.

Kitchen gadgets

I love kitchen gadgets and seem to have them stuffed into every nook and cranny in my kitchen. When I moved house I realized just how many I had collected and shockingly discovered that many of them were unused and still had their tags attached! There are a few that I turn to time and time again to make my life simpler, and I know if I didn't have them I would have to work a lot harder in the kitchen.

SPICE BOX
I don't know what I would do without my spice box: the perfect, compact place to store those little gems of flavor. Not only will storing spices in a box or canister help them stay fresher for longer, but keeping them together allows you to free up much-needed space in that overflowing pantry. To find out what I keep in my spice box, *see* pages 37–41.

SPICE GRINDER
Some spices can't be ground easily in a pestle and mortar, such as cinnamon sticks and nutmeg. If you want to get into making your own garam masalas (*see* page 171) then you need to grind spices to a fine powder, which requires a lot of elbow grease. I bought my spice grinder quite cheaply and it hasn't failed me yet.

PESTLE & MORTAR
Every kitchen needs a pestle and mortar, if only for somewhere to drop your keys when you walk into the kitchen! I use my pestle and mortar for bashing, grinding, mixing, blending and a whole lot more. It's my favorite kitchen tool and I couldn't live without it.

There are so many fancy pestle and mortars out there, but I like my good old heavy granite one. You can use a food processor instead but I prefer to grind my spices by hand so I can check how coarse they are.

MICROPLANE GRATER
It is so much easier to grate garlic, ginger and citrus rind on a Microplane than on a standard grater.

MINI CHOPPER/MINI FOOD PROCESSOR

Some ingredients need to be chopped very fine, which is great if you have good knife skills. If you want to cut your time in half it's best to pop them in a mini chopper and let the machine do all the work for you. It's great for pureeing tomatoes, onions, garlic and ginger and for making quick pastes and marinades.

IMMERSION BLENDER

A nice-to-have, not a must-have, kitchen gadget that has more uses than you may think. I usually use mine to blitz veggies and lentils after cooking. I like the way using an immersion blender allows you to control the texture of the final dish. For example, you can make your soups and dhal as smooth or as chunky as you like. I suggest using an immersion blender for my Spiced Vegetable Soup with Lentils & Roasted Chile and my Black Dhal (*see* pages 100 and 140.)

SMALL ROLLING PIN

You can easily use a large rolling pin for making Indian breads such as rotis and parathas (*see* pages 144 and 149) but I prefer to use a traditional thin Indian one. My first kitchen gift was a small rolling pin and board for helping my grandmother make fresh rotis for dinner. My habits haven't changed and I love the control you have with a small pin—and it's also easier to store.

ELECTRIC WHISK

This is another nice-to-have gadget, and certainly not essential in an Indian kitchen. I love to bake and I use my electric whisk a lot, but you can easily use a balloon whisk and a little muscle if you have time and are feeling strong.

CHAPTER

5

BBQ INDIAN SUMMER

SERVES 4
Prep time 10 minutes,
plus (preferably) chilling
Cook time 10 minutes

1 tbsp vegetable oil
1 tsp cumin seeds
3 scallions, finely sliced
3 garlic cloves, finely chopped
2 dried red chiles, soaked in boiling
 water for 5 minutes, then drained
 and finely chopped
2 tsp garam masala
1–1 1/4 lb ground beef
grated zest of 1 orange
1 egg, beaten
2 tbsp soft bread crumbs—stale
 white bread is preferable but any
 will do, including naan (optional)
good pinch of sea salt and pepper
4 burger buns, to serve

Beet and carrot slaw
1 raw beet, grated
1 carrot, grated
1 tsp horseradish sauce
2 tbsp plain Greek yogurt
juice of 1/2 lemon, or to taste
good pinch of sea salt and pepper,
 or to taste

Blazing burgers

You can't have a barbecue without a burger, and I don't mean regular boring burgers that are crying out for some life. I mean delicious, juicy, flavor-filled ones. And you have to have some slaw to go with it.

· MY SECRET ·
Sometimes I stuff my burgers with a little cheese, such as mozzarella or blue cheese. It melts perfectly in the middle of the burger and oozes out as you bite in.

Gently heat the oil in a skillet and add the cumin seeds. When they are sizzling, stir in the scallions, garlic and chiles and fry for 30 seconds before stirring in the garam masala. Turn off the heat and allow the garam masala to cook in the residual heat.

In the meantime, mix together the beef, orange zest, egg, bread crumbs (if using) and salt and pepper in a bowl. Add the fried spices and mix well. Form into burger shapes and pop in the fridge for 30 minutes to firm up, if you have time.

Make the slaw by mixing all the ingredients together in a serving bowl. Taste and adjust the seasoning.

Cook the burgers in a preheated griddle pan or on an outdoor grill, or in a broiler preheated to high, for a few minutes on each side, flipping them often, or until cooked through to your liking. Serve them inside a burger bun topped with slaw, along with your favorite burger extras.

SERVES 4
Prep time 5 minutes
Cook time 45 minutes

$1\frac{1}{4}$–$1\frac{1}{2}$ lb new potatoes,
    halved if really large
1 tsp cumin seeds
1 tsp coriander seeds
1 dried red chile
2 tbsp Mango Chutney (*see* page 167)
2 tbsp vegetable oil
a few rosemary sprigs
good pinch of sea salt, or to taste,
    plus extra (optional) for sprinkling

Glazed baby potatoes

*I devised this dish when I
had to visit Norway for work.
I needed to come up with
something that I could prepare
in advance and that would
be very different from what the
people of the country would
normally experience. It tastes
sensational, so definitely give
this a go if you fancy mixing
up your roast potatoes recipe.*

Preheat an outdoor grill to medium-high or the oven to 400°F.

Fill a saucepan with cold water, add the potatoes and bring to a boil,
then cook for about 15 minutes, or until cooked through.

Drain the potatoes in a colander and shake them well. Try to rough
up the edges as these will go crispy when roasted.

In the meantime, make the glaze. Coarsely crush the cumin,
coriander seeds and chile with a pestle and mortar. Mix the rest
of the ingredients together and add the spices. Taste and adjust
the seasoning.

Rub the glaze over the potatoes, wrap in foil and bake on the
outdoor grill with the lid closed or in the oven for about 30 minutes.
Serve sprinkled with a little extra salt if you like.

SERVES 4
Prep time 10 minutes
Cook time 35–45 minutes

8 –12 chicken drumsticks
lemon wedges, for squeezing over

Sticky chicken marinade
3 tbsp barbecue sauce—
   I like the hickory ones
2 tbsp soy sauce
2 tbsp honey
3 scallions, finely chopped
3 garlic cloves, finely chopped
1 tbsp peeled and finely chopped
   fresh ginger
1–2 fresh red chiles, finely chopped
2 tbsp finely chopped cilantro

Harissa, mint & cumin marinade
2 tbsp plain Greek yogurt
3 tbsp harissa

3 tbsp finely chopped mint
2 tbsp olive oil
2 tsp cumin seeds, roughly crushed
   with a pestle and mortar
2 tsp honey
juice of 1 lemon

Rosemary, cilantro & garlic marinade
4 garlic cloves, finely chopped
a few rosemary sprigs,
   roughly chopped
3 tbsp roughly chopped cilantro
3 tsp coriander seeds, roughly
   crushed with a pestle and mortar
3 tbsp olive oil
good pinch of sea salt and pepper

Chicken drummers

I couldn't pick just one recipe, so I have shared three of my favorite marinades. If you have time, then these taste best when they have been able to marinate, so cover them and chill in the fridge for at least a few hours. But don't worry if you haven't the time—they will still taste delicious.

Make a few deep slashes in the drumsticks so that the flavors go right to the core.

Mix your chosen marinade ingredients together and rub all over the chicken in a glass or ceramic baking dish. Cover and leave to marinate in the fridge if you have time.

When ready to cook the drumsticks, cook over a preheated outdoor grill for about 35 minutes, or place in a roasting tray and cook in an oven preheated to 400°F for 40 to 45 minutes, or until cooked through. Serve with lemon wedges.

FOLLOWING PAGE:
Top left: Sticky chicken marinade
Bottom left: Rosemary,
cilantro & garlic marinade
Bottom right: Harissa,
mint & cumin marinade

SERVES 4
Prep time 15 minutes
Cook time 5 minutes

2 eggs
1 tsp chile powder
1 tsp garlic paste
$1/2$ tsp ground turmeric
$1/2$ tsp black peppercorns,
   crushed with a pestle
   and mortar
good pinch of sea salt

3 tbsp all-purpose flour
$1^1/_2$ cups dried unsweetened coconut
$1^1/_2$ cups panko bread crumbs
20 raw jumbo shrimp, shells
   removed but tails left on, deveined
2 tbsp vegetable oil
juice of 1 lime, plus extra lime
   wedges for squeezing over

Coconut-crusted shrimp

I have always been fond of seafood and it seems to taste so much better on the grill. The shrimp can be cooked in a skillet placed on the grill or on skewers, it really doesn't make too much difference which method you use. If using wooden skewers, soak them in water for 30 minutes before using or they will burst into flames over the barbecue. I am using a mix of panko (Japanese-style) bread crumbs as well as dried unsweetened coconut to bread the shrimp, but you can easily use regular bread crumbs instead.

Beat the eggs with the chile powder, garlic paste, turmeric, crushed peppercorns and salt in a bowl. Put the flour in a separate bowl. Mix the coconut and bread crumbs together in another bowl.

Bread the shrimp by tossing them in the flour, making sure they are evenly coated, then dipping them in the egg mixture and then rolling them in the bread crumbs. It's best if you double-bread them, so dip them again in the egg and then again in bread crumbs.

Preheat an outdoor grill to medium heat.

If cooking in a skillet, gently heat the pan on a cool part of the grill. Add the oil and then fry the shrimp for a few minutes on each side. Once they are crispy and golden brown, drain on paper towels. If cooking on skewers, carefully skewer the shrimp, trying not to lose too many bread crumbs. Drizzle over the oil and cook over the flames, turning often, until crispy and golden brown.

Squeeze over the lime juice just before serving, with some extra wedges for lime lovers.

SERVES 4
Prep time 5 minutes,
plus marinating
Cook time up to 15 minutes

Marinade
3 tbsp vegetable oil or light
   olive oil
1 tsp cumin seeds
1 tsp ground coriander
1 tsp ground turmeric
$\frac{1}{2}$ tsp chile powder, or to taste
1 fresh red chile, finely chopped
   (optional)

2 fat garlic cloves, finely chopped
a few rosemary sprigs,
   roughly chopped
good pinch of sea salt and pepper,
   or to taste

12 lamb chops, French-trimmed
   if possible or trimmed of any fat
lime wedges, for squeezing over

Finger-licking chops

Lamb chops marinated in spices and rosemary—it says it all. One of my fondest memories is of munching on lamb chops when I visited family during my year traveling around the world after studying. I had spent all that time with people I'd never met, and happiness overcame me when my parents told me there were members of our family living in a remote part of Australia. It was barbecue season and they decided to present me with dish after dish of delicious food I had truly missed. I have been generous with the chile, but you can reduce it if you aren't that keen.

Mix all the marinade ingredients together—you can add a little water if you need the marinade to go farther. Taste and adjust the seasoning and heat if you think it needs it.

Rub the marinade all over the lamb chops in a dish, then cover and pop in the fridge to marinate for a few hours, if you have time.

When you are ready, cook the chops on a hot outdoor grill or under a broiler preheated to high, in batches, for up to 4 minutes on each side, or until cooked to your liking. I like my lamb pink, so I cook it for only 2 minutes on each side. Serve with lime wedges and some sides for a wonderful Indian summer feast.

SERVES 4
Prep time 5 minutes
Cook time 10–12 minutes
for fillets; 25–30 minutes
for a side of salmon

Spice paste
4 tbsp coconut cream (the creamy
    top layer of a can of coconut milk
    will work, or use grated fresh
    coconut if you find some)
2 tbsp plain Greek yogurt
2 tbsp finely chopped cilantro
1 tbsp tamarind paste, or to taste
small handful of fresh curry leaves
    (see My Secret, page 20) (optional)
1 tsp black mustard seeds
1/2 tsp ground turmeric

1 fresh red chile, seeded if you
    wish, sliced
1 tbsp peeled and julienned
    fresh ginger
good pinch of salt, or to taste—
    this dish has coastal flavors,
    so I prefer sea salt, but you
    can use regular table salt

4 salmon fillets, about 6 oz each,
    or 1 large side of salmon,
    1 1/4–1 1/2 lb

Scented steamed fish

This recipe was inspired by a trip I made to the idyllic Indian spice state of Kerala when I became really serious about cooking. I traveled around with my mum learning about spices—the first of many spice trips we went on together. Some of the best seafood dishes hail from this region and they are packed full of native spices and herbs. A traditional way to cook coastal dishes is in banana leaves, which grow in abundance in Kerala and which I've been told are available in some Asian stores. If you haven't got any at hand (and I rarely have), then just use some parchment paper soaked in a little water. This will keep the fish moist and won't catch fire on the barbecue.

Mix all the spice paste ingredients together in a bowl. Taste and add a little more salt or tamarind if you think it needs it.

Rub the paste all over the fish, then wrap the fish in parchment paper or foil.

Cook over an ourdoor grill preheated to medium or in an oven preheated to 350°F for 10 to 12 minutes, depending on the thickness of the fillets, or for 25 to 30 minutes if cooking a whole side of salmon. The salmon tastes best when it is slightly pink in the middle, so it's advisable to undercook it if you aren't sure. You can always pop it back on the grill or into the oven if you need to. Serve with some delicious sides and salads.

· MY SECRET ·
The tamarind adds a sweet
and sour flavor to the fish, but
if you can't lay your hands on
any, add some freshly
squeezed lime juice and
sugar instead.

SERVES 4
Prep time 15 minutes,
plus (preferably) chilling
Cook time 10 minutes

1 lb ground lamb
4 sun-dried tomatoes in oil,
    drained and finely chopped
1 tsp garam masala
1 tsp ground turmeric
1/2 tbsp fennel seeds
1 tsp cumin seeds
3 garlic cloves, finely chopped
1 tbsp peeled and finely chopped
    fresh ginger

1–2 fresh red chiles, finely chopped
grated zest and juice of 1 lemon
2 tbsp finely chopped cilantro
3 tbsp finely chopped mint leaves
2 tsp honey
good pinch of sea salt
long woody rosemary sprigs, for
    skewering, bottom leaves removed
lemon wedges, for squeezing over

Herby lamb kebabs

*You can find lamb kebabs
everywhere. The best I've ever
had was at a family wedding
in Baroda in Gujarat. They
were succulent, perfectly spiced
and loaded with herbs. This
is a recipe I created not long
after I returned and I've been
making them ever since. The
sun-dried tomatoes add a
summer vibe. If you can't
find woody rosemary to use
as skewers, you can use metal
or even wooden ones. Just
make sure you soak the
wooden ones in water for
around 30 minutes before
using or they may catch fire!*

Mix all the ingredients except the lemon juice, rosemary sprigs and lemon wedges together in a bowl.

Press the meat mixture onto the woody ends of the rosemary sprigs and pop in the fridge for 30 minutes to firm up, if you have time.

On an outdoor grill preheated to medium, or in a griddle pan over medium heat, or under a broiler preheated to medium, cook the kebabs for about 10 minutes, squeezing over the lemon juice while cooking and turning often, or until cooked through. Serve with lemon wedges, along with some Cucumber Raita (*see* page 166) to cool down any chile heat.

· MY SECRET ·
You can use ground
pork, turkey or beef
instead of lamb. Using
the grated zest and juice
of an orange instead of a
lemon adds a different
citrus note.

Dad went to India on a spice-buying trip and came back with his most treasured spice of all—my mum. They were married three months later. Loving the outfit, Dad!

Mum on her wedding day, looking stunning.

Dad was always proud of the Patak's factory and never missed a moment to show off his and Mum's new recipe creations.

How '80s does this look?! When Mum joined the family business she soon became the face of Patak's and worked tirelessly developing new recipes, some of which are still sold today—you've gotta love our Tandoori Paste. I used to see this poster above reception at the office when I was young.

Mum's grandparents (and dog) lived in Mumbai, but were both born in Ahmedabad, Gujarat. Mum learned a lot of her cooking skills from her grandmother.

Dad on one of his business trips checking produce. He was meticulous and always kept a close eye on the quality of each and every ingredient that was used in the Patak's secret recipes.

SERVES 4
Prep time 2 minutes
Cook time 10 minutes

4 large ears of corn, preferably
   in their husks
2 tbs butter, softened
1 tsp crushed red pepper flakes or
   1 fresh red chile, finely chopped,
   or to taste

good pinch of sea salt, or to taste,
   and pepper
grated zest and juice of 1 lime,
   or to taste

Scorched corn on the cob

This has to be one of the easiest recipes to make. It uses only a few ingredients yet tastes absolutely divine; you just can't beat corn being charred on a barbecue and brushed liberally with butter and chile. You can find street vendors selling corn in their husks all over Asia and each area will have its own unique way of adding regional flair to it. I drew inspiration for this recipe from the beaches of Mumbai, where you can get some of the very best corn on the cob I've ever tried. If you can find corn cobs in their husks, then perfect, but pre-shucked corn on the cob is absolutely fine to use.

Scorch the ears of corn on an outdoor grill preheated to high, turning often, until they are charred.

In the meantime, make the basting butter by mixing the rest of the ingredients except the lime zest together. Give it a taste and add more chile, salt or lime juice if you think it needs it.

Once the husks are nicely charred, carefully peel them back to reveal the cobs. Baste the corn cobs with the flavored butter often and continue to cook until the kernels are tender and starting to color evenly. Serve with extra flavored butter and sprinkled with the lime zest.

· MY SECRET ·
If you have any leftovers, cut the corn off the cob and reheat in a smoking-hot pan for a few minutes. Toss in some fresh cilantro and a squeeze of lime, and you have a quick corn salsa: great with nachos.

SERVES 4
Prep time 10 minutes
Cook time 1 hour 10 minutes

Dry rub
1 tbsp fennel seeds
1 tsp cumin seeds
1 tsp black peppercorns
1 tbsp smoked paprika

$3^1/_4$–$3^1/_2$ lb pork belly ribs, individual
   ribs or as a rack—try
   to get to the butcher for these
   for the best-quality meat
$1/_3$ cup plus 1 tbsp apple juice

Marinade
1 cup tomato puree
2 tbsp golden syrup (such as Lyle's)
   or maple syrup
1 tbsp Worcestershire sauce
2 tsp spicy brown mustard
1 tsp fresh or dried oregano, finely
   chopped
1 tsp finely chopped garlic
$1/_4$ cup apple juice
sea salt and pepper

Smokin' ribs

Ribs are always a favorite at barbecues, and the key is in the marinade. If you have a smoker, then fire it up to really intensify the flavor. If you haven't, fear not because smoked paprika has a magical way of making everything taste like you did! This recipe has wo parts: the dry rub, which is baked onto the ribs in the oven, and then the wet marinade, which is basted on when finishing them off on the grill. If the weather isn't playing ball, instead of basting the meat with the marinade, just pour it all over the ribs and pop them under the broiler to char them.

Preheat the oven to 300°F.

Using a pestle and mortar, bash the fennel and cumin seeds and peppercorns together for the dry rub. Stir in the smoked paprika and rub the spice mix all over the ribs. Place them in a roasting tray so that they fit in a single layer. Pour in the apple juice, cover tightly with foil and bake for 1 hour.

In the meantime, gently heat all the marinade ingredients in a saucepan. Taste and adjust the seasoning if you think it needs it. Reserve some of it to serve as a dipping sauce.

After an hour the ribs will be tender, so it's time to move to the barbecue. Smother the meat with some of the remaining marinade and place directly on the rack of an outdoor grill preheated to high. Cook for 10 minutes, moving them around and basting with the marinade as often as you can. Serve the ribs with potato wedges, pickled veggies and the reserved marinade for dipping.

SERVES 4
Prep time 5 minutes
Cook time 2 minutes

Spice rubs, pastes & oil

Everyone needs some good spice rubs and pastes up their sleeve, and ideally ones that will go with a whole host of meats, seafood and veggies. I grew up learning all about garam masalas and which spices taste best with which ingredients. Our spice pastes have become legendary and I've picked up several secret tips along the way, especially when I used to do the spice grinding for the family products. Over the years I have bent a lot of these rules, so here are a few special spicing ideas of mine for you to try out when the barbecue season comes around. And as with all my recipes, if you haven't got an ingredient or two, then don't worry about it. Just use what you have and see how it turns out.

1 tsp coriander seeds
1 tsp cumin seeds
1 dried red chile
$1/4$ tsp black peppercorns
$1/2$ tsp ground turmeric
good pinch of ground cinnamon
good pinch of ground cloves
(optional)
good pinch of sea salt
$1/2$ tsp your favorite dried
herbs (rosemary and mint
work well with lamb;
oregano with chicken)

Dry rub for meat

This basic rub works wonderfully with most meats. If you are going to have it with chicken, I suggest adding a little more coriander seed, and if using with lamb, then add a small quantity of fennel seeds. I like to toast my spices first but don't worry if you don't have time. It just releases more of the flavor. Gently massage the rub into your favorite meat and roast in the oven or on the barbecue.

Gently heat a heavy-bottomed skillet and toast the coriander and cumin seeds, chile and peppercorns for a few minutes until fragrant and the seeds are golden brown.

Pour into a mortar and allow to cool for a few minutes, then grind well with a pestle. Toss in the remaining spices, salt and herbs and mix together. This dry spice rub will keep in an airtight container for a few weeks.

Wet paste for meat

To make the dry rub for meat into a paste, just add 1 teaspoon each crushed garlic and peeled and grated fresh ginger with a little vegetable or canola oil. This will keep happily in an airtight container in the fridge for at least 5 days.

Wet paste for seafood

1 tsp fennel seeds
1/2 tsp black mustard seeds
1/4 tsp cumin seeds
1/4 tsp ground turmeric
2 tbsp coconut cream (the creamy top layer of a can of coconut milk will work) or 1 tbsp dried unsweetened coconut and 1 tbsp plain Greek yogurt
1 tsp garlic paste
1 tsp tamarind paste (optional)
grated zest and juice of 1 lime
good pinch of sea salt, or to taste, and pepper
pinch of sugar (optional)

Making a paste for coating seafood is a great way to enhance their delicate flavors. I borrow southern Indian ingredients to create a simple paste that is perfect for all types of seafood. Rub on your favorite seafood and roast in the oven or on the barbecue.

Mix all the ingredients together and taste. Add more salt and even a pinch of sugar to balance it out if you think it needs it.

Put into an airtight container, pop in the fridge and use within 3 days.

Spiced oil for veggies

2–3 tbsp olive oil
1/2 tsp cumin seeds
1/4 tsp coriander seeds
good pinch of crushed red pepper flakes
1/4 tsp ground turmeric
good pinch of sea salt and pepper

I love vegetables just as they are, but adding this spiced oil to them can make them taste truly exciting. Simply rub on your chosen veggies and then roast in the oven or on the barbecue.

Mix all the ingredients together and put into an airtight container. This infused oil will keep for around a month.

Fridge favorites

There are a few essential fresh ingredients that I like to keep on hand to help me lift the flavor of my dishes. The fresher the better.

THE HOLY TRINITY— GARLIC, GINGER & FRESH CHILES

I don't think I need to explain why these three ingredients are so important. I don't know what I would do without fresh garlic, ginger and chiles in my life. As well as using them chopped, I also like to grate them and make my own garlic and ginger paste (puree)— easy peasy with a mini chopper/food processor (*see* page 111).

If I know I am going away and have any of these left in my fridge, I grate them into separate ice cube trays, topping each compartment with water and then a thin layer of oil before freezing. Then, whenever I need them, I simply pop out a cube. I also freeze my chiles in an airtight bag and chop them from frozen.

There are so many different types of chiles and all freeze well—see what I've written about my favorite ones on pages 88–9.

When buying fresh garlic, look closely to see if it has roots growing out of the top. If it does it means it's old and won't taste fresh.

Ginger should be heavy and the skin shouldn't be wrinkly. Break a little off and check it feels moist, as it will last so much longer if it does.

CILANTRO

Although you can grow this easily I have never had much luck and so I buy cilantro bunches and keep them in my fridge. To keep it looking fresh and bright, wrap the stalks in some damp paper towels. Try with Avocado & Cilantro Salsa (*see* page 25).

CURRY LEAVES

I grew up with a fresh curry leaf plant in my kitchen so we were never short of fresh curry leaves. You can buy them dried but I'm not a fan and prefer to leave them out if I don't have fresh leaves on hand. When you do find them, make sure you buy a few extra bunches and pop them in the freezer. They freeze amazingly well and you will have them when you need them. Be sure to always thoroughly wash them under clean, cold running water before adding to recipes or freezing.

Crisped up in a little oil, fresh curry leaves make a wonderful garnish for topping many spiced dishes. Try with Charred Baby Eggplants or Salty Masala Lassi (*see* pages 20 and 205).

ONIONS

I go through onions like you wouldn't believe. I always keep scallions and red onions in my fridge for raw dishes, and I use white or brown onions for cooking. I'm sure I don't need to tell you that if they are sprouting roots, you have held onto them too long.

Transform the humble onion into Carrot, Onion & Spinach Bhajias or a versatile Caramelized Onion & Balsamic Chutney (*see* pages 14 and 161).

YOGURT

My grandmother used to make her own yogurt, which always tasted better than what we could buy, but I never make my own and so plain Greek yogurt is on my shopping list every week.

Yogurt is great as a healthy thickener as well as a good substitute for cream in those indulgent desserts, including Pomegranate & Ricotta Frozen Yogurt (*see* page 190). You can mix it with other ingredients to transform it into a tasty dressing for salads, or drizzle it unadulterated on spiced, savory dishes, such as Papri Chaat (*see* page 30). It is also a key ingredient in classic Cucumber Raita (*see* page 166).

LEMON/LIME

I like to balance the flavor of a lot of my recipes with some citrus and always have lemons and limes on hand. Their juice and zesty flavor brings out the spice flavors in a way I can't explain.

CHAPTER

6

THOSE LITTLE
EXTRAS

SERVES 4 TO 6
Prep time 10 minutes,
plus soaking
Cook time 2 hours

· MY SECRET ·
Mash boiled lentils
with the back of a spoon
or pulse a few times using an
immersion blender. It will
make the dish a little
creamier, especially if you
stir through some yogurt
at the end.

7 oz dried black urad dhal
(black lentils)
2 small onions or large shallots,
finely sliced
1 tsp ground turmeric
4 black cardamom pods (optional)
1 cinnamon stick
2–3 fresh Indian finger chiles or
jalapeños, slit down the middle
but left whole
3 tbsp vegetable oil (this recipe tastes
best made with ghee/clarified
butter—do as you wish)
2 tsp cumin seeds

2 fat garlic cloves, finely chopped
1 tbsp peeled and julienned fresh
ginger
2 tsp coriander seeds
1/2 tsp ground asafetida/hing
(see page 41) (optional)
2 tbsp tomato paste
10 cherry tomatoes, cut in half
good pinch of sea salt, or to taste

To garnish
lots of chopped cilantro
a few tbsp plain Greek yogurt

Black dhal

I'm all about the shortcuts
and love creating meals that
are simple and quick. However,
this recipe is not one of those.
It's a labor of love, but it truly is
worth all the effort. The best
black dhal (lentils) I've ever had
(rumored to be the best in the
world) was from the Bukhara
restaurant in Delhi. They say
they cook it for over 40 hours—
no wonder it tastes so good!
Oh, and they add a lot more fat
than I have here. I don't have
40 hours and so this will never
taste as good as theirs, but it
sure hits the spot when I'm
craving it.

You can find black urad dhal,
or black lentils, at all Asian
shops and I do recommend that
you hunt it out. Sadly there
really isn't a suitable substitute.

Soak the lentils overnight (or for at least 8 hours) in plenty of cold
water. The next day, drain off the water and rinse again a few times
until the water runs clear. Pour the lentils into a saucepan with
plenty of cold water (around 4 cups will do) and add half the onions
or shallots, the turmeric, black cardamoms (if using), cinnamon
stick and chiles. Bring to a boil, then reduce the heat and allow to
simmer for 1 1/2 hours, or until the lentils are tender, topping up
with more water if necessary.

Make the tadka—the scented oil that adds flavor to the dhal—by
gently heating the oil in a skillet and adding half the cumin seeds.
When they are sizzling, stir in the garlic, ginger and remaining
onions or shallots. Cook for 2 minutes while you finely crush the
remaining cumin seeds and the coriander seeds with a pestle and
mortar. Stir this into the skillet with the asafetida/hing (if using),
tomato paste and tomatoes. Add a splash of water, stir well and
allow the spices to cook for a few minutes.

Pour the tadka into the cooked dhal. Add a really good pinch of salt
and bubble for 5 minutes to release the tadka flavors. Taste and
adjust the seasoning if you need to. You can add more chile if you
like yours hot.

Serve garnished with lots of cilantro and a little yogurt.

SERVES 4
Prep time 5 minutes
Cook time 30 minutes

1¹/₄–1¹/₂ lb carrots, cut into halves or quarters lengthwise, depending on the thickness of your carrots
2 tbsp olive oil
1 tsp caraway seeds
good pinch of sea salt

good pinch of cracked black peppercorns
a few thyme sprigs— I love lemon thyme
1 tsp unsalted butter
good drizzle of honey

Caraway glazed carrots

This dish used to make a regular appearance at Sunday lunch when I was a kid. My dad would take us all for a bike ride and then we would spend what was left of the morning cooling off at the local swimming pool. We would return home just in time to see my mum putting the finishing touches on family lunch before tucking into a well-deserved meal. After a snooze on the sofa it was time for dessert. I miss Sundays with my family . . . but at least I can re-create the dishes to bring back the memories. If you can't lay your hands on caraway seeds, use cumin or coriander seeds to add a little earthiness to the dish.

Preheat the oven to 400°F.

Mix all the ingredients except the honey together, spread out in a roasting tray and roast for about 25 minutes, or until soft and crisping up at the edges.

Drizzle over the honey and roast for a further 5 minutes. Perfect with any roast dinner or as a side dish to any meal.

MAKES 8
Prep time 10 minutes,
plus proofing
Cook time around 15 minutes

2 cups whole wheat flour (chapati atta), plus extra for dusting
2 tbsp vegetable oil
good pinch of sea salt

around ⅓ cup plus 1 tbsp warm water
butter or ghee (clarified butter), for brushing (optional)

· MY SECRET ·
Sometimes I brush my rotis with flavored butter—I love garlic and coriander butter and also rosemary and chile butter.

Classic roti

I grew up with fresh hot rotis (also known as chapatis), and I've been making them ever since I was little. A roti is a traditional unleavened bread from northern India, cooked in a dry pan. It can then be brushed with butter or ghee (clarified butter) if you want to be indulgent. This recipe uses a multigrain flour, called chapati atta, available from all Asian shops. If you can't find it, just use whole wheat flour; if you wish, you can sprinkle in a little all-purpose flour to lighten it up. This is a great basic dough, which means it's perfect for adding flavors and spices to. My recipe is classically plain.

Mix the flour, oil and salt together in a large bowl. Pour in enough of the warm water to make a dough. The dough shouldn't be sticky or dry. Knead for a few minutes on a lightly floured work surface and then return the dough to the bowl, cover with plastic wrap and allow to rest for 30 minutes.

Heat a large, heavy-bottomed skillet over a fairly high heat and start rolling out the rotis. Divide the dough into 8 equal pieces. Sprinkle your work surface and rolling pin with a little more flour. Roll each dough ball into a circle about ⅛ inch thick. Sprinkle the dough with more flour if it begins to stick. Dust off any excess flour from a roti and place it in the pan. When little bubbles form on the top, flip the roti over to cook the other side. Use a spatula or rolled-up clean kitchen towel to press the roti against the heat of the pan.

Once the roti is golden brown on both sides, transfer to a warm plate and brush with butter or ghee, if you wish—there is no need to premelt it, as it will melt when it touches the hot roti. Cover with a clean kitchen towel while you make the rest. There's nothing like fresh hot bread, so serve these immediately.

SERVES 4
Prep time 10 minutes
Cook time 35–40 minutes

2 tbsp light olive oil
2 tsp garam masala
1/4 tsp crushed red pepper flakes
2 heaped tbsp soft white bread
   crumbs
2 garlic cloves, finely chopped

juice of 1/2 lemon
7 oz cauliflower, broken into florets
   (31/2–4 cups)
101/2 oz broccoli, broken into florets
   (51/4–6 cups)
good pinch of sea salt and pepper

· MY SECRET ·
Any robust greens
work well here, so try
adding Brussels sprouts,
cut in half, to bring
some extra nuttiness to
your side dish.

Crunchy roast cauliflower & broccoli

*I love this recipe. Roast
cauliflower and broccoli
with ingredients they
love and they will taste
just amazing.*

Preheat the oven to 400°F.

Mix all the ingredients together and spread out on a rimmed baking sheet in a single layer. Roast for 35 to 40 minutes until crunchy and starting to color around the edges. Make sure you scoop up all the crispy roasted bread crumbs before serving with your favorite Big Bite (*see* pages 44–66).

SERVES 4
Prep time 5 minutes
Cook time 45 minutes

2 lb roasting potatoes (any will do),
    cut into large bite-size pieces

Spice paste
1 tbsp cumin seeds
2 tsp coriander seeds
1/2 tsp black peppercorns

2 dried red chiles
2 fat garlic cloves, peeled
good pinch of sea salt
4 tbsp oil—canola oil or light
    olive oil is great

· MY SECRET ·
You can make extra
spice paste and keep
it in your fridge for about
a week. If you omit the
garlic, it will keep for
about a month.

Cumin roast potatoes

*These are roasties with a
difference. If you have any
leftover spice pastes rolling
around in your cupboards,
then this is perfect for using
them up and adding some
extra flavor to an all-time
favorite. One of the best
bits of a roast dinner is the
potatoes, especially if they are
crispy on the outside and fluffy
on the inside. Every Sunday
my mother would make these
using one of our spice pastes,
but if you don't have any on
hand, then here is a paste you
can easily make up yourself.*

Preheat the oven to 400°F.

Fill a large saucepan with cold water, add the potatoes and bring
to a boil, then cook for around 20 minutes, or until soft.

In the meantime, make the spice paste. Coarsely crush the cumin
and coriander seeds, peppercorns and chiles with a pestle and
mortar. Add the garlic cloves and sea salt and pound together,
then work in half the oil to make a paste.

Drain the potatoes in a colander and rough them up so that the
edges will go really crispy in the oven. Put a large roasting tray
(large enough so that the potatoes will sit in a single layer) directly
on the burner, add the remaining oil and gently heat before tipping
in the potatoes. Stir well and leave for 1 minute, then turn off the
heat and add the spice paste. Toss the potatoes well to coat, then
transfer the tray to the oven to crisp up for around 20 minutes.

SERVES 4
Prep time 2 minutes,
plus soaking
Cook time 10 minutes

1½ cups white basmati rice,
rinsed in several changes of
water and left to soak in cold
water for around 30 minutes
if you have time
1 cinnamon stick
1 blade of mace (optional)
2 Indian bay leaves

4 cloves
4 green cardamom pods
1 tsp cumin seeds
2 black cardamom pods (optional)
good pinch of saffron threads
(optional)
good pinch of sea salt
2 tbsp vegetable oil

Foolproof pilau rice

*Cooking rice always worries
people. There are two main
ways of getting perfect rice:
either letting the rice absorb
every drop of water, or draining
off any excess once it's cooked.
Personally, I prefer the latter,
as it works every time and you
never have to deal with burnt rice
stuck to the bottom of your pan.*

*I'm using basmati rice for its
flavor and the heavenly scent that
fills my kitchen during cooking. If
you have time, soak the grains for
half an hour. It allows them to
lengthen so that you maximize
their beautiful flavor, but don't
leave them any longer, as they
will soften too much and break
up when you boil them. You can
use this as a base recipe and add
lots of different spices or leave it
plain if you prefer.*

Fill a saucepan with plenty of cold water and bring it to a boil. Drain
the rice and add it to the water with all the spices and salt.
Stir well and pour in the oil. Stir again before leaving it to cook
for 7 minutes, or until al dente—it should have a little bite to it.

Drain off the water and allow the rice to steam for a minute in the
colander or sieve. If you aren't serving it right away, then a foolproof
way of keeping it fluffy and hot is to put some foil over the sieve.
Pour some water into the rice pan and put the sieve on top. Gently
heat the water and leave the rice to steam until you are ready for it.

· MY SECRET ·
Depending on what I am eating
my rice with, I like to use different oils
such as sesame oil, coconut oil or even
mustard oil to complement the flavors
of the main dish. I may also stir through
some coconut milk to make my rice
creamy, which goes great with
Thai dishes.

MAKES 8
Prep time 20 minutes,
plus proofing
Cook time 20 minutes

2 cups whole wheat flour (chapati atta—*see* page 144), plus extra for dusting
2 tbsp finely chopped mint leaves
1 tsp cumin seeds
1/2 tsp chile powder, or more if you love yours hot
2 fat garlic cloves, finely chopped

4 tbsp vegetable oil, plus extra for cooking
good pinch of sea salt
around 1/3 cup plus 1 tablespoon warm water
butter or ghee (clarified butter), for brushing (optional)

Flaky mint & chile paratha

Parathas are flaky breads made from whole wheat flour or all-purpose flour. The flaky layers are created by adding oil, butter or ghee (clarified butter) to the dough at different stages. They can be any shape you like, but I'm opting for round. You can leave them plain, add spices and herbs to the dough like I have or even stuff them with spiced veggies (see page 150). Personally, I prefer adding a few simple ingredients to give the bread some life, and then dipping it into a fresh hot chai (see page 213). My ideal weekend breakfast.

Mix together the flour, mint, cumin, chile powder, garlic, most of the oil and the salt in a large bowl. Pour in enough of the warm water to make a dough. The dough shouldn't be sticky or dry. Knead for a few minutes on a lightly floured work surface and then return to the bowl, cover with plastic wrap and allow to rest for 30 minutes.

Divide the dough into 8 equal pieces. Sprinkle your work surface and rolling pin with a little more flour and roll each dough ball into a circle about 1/8 inch thick. Sprinkle the dough with more flour if it begins to stick. Brush a little of the remaining oil on top of the dough and roll up into a cigar shape. Grab one end, lift the dough up and slap it onto the work surface to lengthen it. Grab the other end and do the same until it is around 20 inches long. Rub a little more oil over the dough and roll it up so that it looks like a coil, tucking the ends into the middle to hold its shape. Brush the top with a little more oil and allow to rest while you do the same with the other dough balls.

Sprinkle your work surface with a little flour and roll each coil to flatten them out into circles a little thicker than last time. If you have time, you can now repeat the rolling, lengthening, oiling, coiling and flattening process—each time you do this you add more layers, which will result in extra-flaky parathas.

>>>

Heat a large, heavy-bottomed skillet over medium heat. Dust off any excess flour from a flattened coil and place it in the pan. When little bubbles form on the top, flip the paratha over to cook the other side. Drizzle a little oil into the pan and use a spatula or rolled-up clean kitchen towel to press the paratha against the heat of the pan. Brush the top with a little more oil and flip back over for 30 seconds.

Once the paratha is golden brown on both sides, transfer to a warm plate and brush with butter or ghee, if you wish. Cover with a clean kitchen towel while you make the rest. If you've added enough oil to your parathas, you should be able to see the layers. You can always scrunch each one up a little to release them.

Stuffed parathas

Making a stuffed paratha is slightly different and it isn't flaky like the plain ones above. Make the stuffing first so that it has time to cool. I love simple stuffings like cabbage and peas, but you can use any cooked veggies. Add some flavor to them when sautéeing, such as ground turmeric, cumin seeds, ground coriander and the usual holy trinity of finely chopped garlic, ginger and chiles. Season to taste and you've got yourself a great stuffing. Make the dough as above and roll out into small disks before placing a good heaped tablespoon of cooled stuffing in the middle. Roll the edges up and press together so that the filling is enclosed within, making sure there are no gaps or your filling will fall out. Carefully roll out into a large circle, trying not to break the dough. Cook the parathas like the plain ones above, adding oil to make them crispy. They're a meal in themselves!

SERVES 4
Prep time 10 minutes
Cook time 45 minutes

2 large sweet potatoes, skins
    left on, scrubbed and cut
    in half lengthwise
1 tbsp vegetable oil
1/2 tsp coriander seeds
good pinch of ground cinnamon
a few thyme sprigs

sea salt and pepper
1 tbsp crème fraîche or plain
    Greek yogurt
2 tbsp soft white bread crumbs—
    I like naan bread crumbs
2 tbsp freshly grated
    Parmesan cheese

Sweet potato mash
with a Parmesan crumb

*Mashed potatoes are one of my
all-time favorite sides and I love
any kind, especially sweet
potato mash. This is a recipe
that is a little more labor
intensive than just boiling the
potatoes and mashing them,
but it is worth the bit of extra
effort, which you will be
thankful for with every bite.
Friends are always impressed
when I pop this on the table
and they never believe me when
I share the recipe, as it's so
simple to make.*

Preheat the oven to 400°F.

Rub the sweet potatoes all over with the oil, coriander seeds,
ground cinnamon, thyme and a good pinch of salt and pepper.
Put on a rimmed baking sheet, cut-side up, and roast in the oven
for 40 minutes, or until soft.

Take the potatoes out of the oven and turn the broiler onto high.
Scoop out all the flesh, trying not to tear the crispy skins, and stir
through the crème fraîche or yogurt. Taste and adjust the seasoning
before putting the potato back in the skins. Scatter over the bread
crumbs and sprinkle over the Parmesan. Put under the broiler for
5 minutes, or until the tops are golden brown and crispy.

SERVES 4
Prep time 10 minutes
Cook time about 50 minutes

· MY SECRET ·
When I'm tired I crave
dhal—it's like a hug in a bowl.
To bulk it out and make it
more of a meal, I stir through
some fresh greens such as
spinach or watercress—
a great way to use
up old veg.

1½ cups dried toor dhal (yellow
   lentils/yellow split peas), rinsed in
   several changes of water
1 tsp ground turmeric
2 black cardamom pods (optional)
3 tbsp vegetable oil
2 cinnamon sticks
4 green cardamom pods
6 cloves
2 tsp black mustard seeds
1 tsp cumin seeds
2 scallions, finely sliced

2–3 chiles, any color, seeded if
   you don't like it fiery, some
   chopped and the rest left whole
2 fat garlic cloves, finely chopped
1 tbsp peeled and finely chopped
   fresh ginger
6 cherry tomatoes, cut in half
good pinch of sea salt, or to taste
1 tsp sugar, or to taste
juice of ½ lemon, or to taste
lots of chopped cilantro, to garnish

Tadka dhal

This is probably the most famous lentil dish coming out of India—yellow lentils tempered with spices and the usual holy trinity of garlic, ginger and chile. It has always been a favorite of mine and it would grace our family dinner table at least once a week when I was growing up. There are lots of different recipes for flavoring the oil (tadka), so play around with your spice pantry and see what you come up with. If you don't have half of these spices, then don't worry; just add a tablespoon of your favorite spice paste and it will taste just as delicious.

Gently boil the lentils in a large saucepan of cold water (around 4 cups will do) and stir in the turmeric and black cardamom pods (if using)—this will add a subtle smoky flavor. Allow to cook for around 45 minutes, or until the lentils have softened and started to break down. Skim off any foam that sits on the top and give the lentils a stir every now and again in case they begin to stick on the bottom. If they boil dry, add more water.

Once the lentils have softened, turn down the heat and make the tadka. Gently heat the oil in a skillet and add the cinnamon sticks, green cardamom pods and cloves. When the cardamoms have turned white and the heads of the cloves have swollen, you are ready to stir in the mustard and cumin seeds. When they are sizzling, stir in the scallions, chiles, garlic and ginger.

After a minute, stir through the tomatoes and turn off the heat. Pour the tadka into the dhal so that it floats on top. This is the traditional way to serve it, with the scented oil sitting on top, but I prefer to stir it through. Season with salt, sugar and lemon juice. Finally, stir through plenty of chopped cilantro and serve with some rice or fresh bread for the ultimate comfort food.

MAKES 6 REGULAR-
SIZE OR 10 SMALL
Prep time 3 hours, including proofing
Cook time 5 minutes per batch

· MY SECRET ·
The secret to
achieving an authentic
result is to get your oven
crazy hot, and I mean
super super hot, as
hot as it will go!

²/₃ cup milk
really good pinch of saffron threads
    (depending on the quality, you may
    need more rather than less)
4 cups all-purpose flour, plus extra for
    dusting
1 tsp baking powder
good pinch of baking soda

pinch of sea salt
1 large egg, lightly beaten
¹/₃ cup plus 1 tbsp plain Greek yogurt
6 tbsp honey
vegetable or canola oil, for greasing
    and drizzling
melted butter or ghee (clarified
    butter), for brushing (optional)

Saffron & honey naan breads

Naan bread is something I grew up with. Dad would bring home all sorts of interesting flavors from work to test out. Some were great, and some not so. Dad would absorb every remark my brothers and I would pass over the table and even ask us how we felt about new ideas. I've had too many naans baked in regular ovens that are so far away from the traditional ones made in a classic tandoor that it put me off making them myself. But I wanted to nail this and thankfully, after much experimentation, I came up with this wonderful recipe. Trust me when I say that it's pretty much like the real naan breads baked in a searingly hot clay oven. I've added saffron and honey for a little sweetness, but leave them out if you want them plain (you needn't heat the milk either).

Infuse the milk with the saffron by gently heating them together in a small saucepan. Once the milk has turned golden, turn off the heat. Mix the flour in a bowl with the baking powder, baking soda and salt.

In another bowl, whisk together the cooled infused milk, beaten egg, yogurt and 5 tablespoons of the honey.

Make a well in the dry ingredients and pour in three quarters of the wet mixture. Mix together, adding more of the wet mixture if you need to until the dough comes together.

Knead the dough on a lightly floured work surface for around 5 minutes until soft and pillowy. Pop into a greased bowl, cover with plastic wrap and leave to double in size. This could take from 30 minutes up to 2 hours, depending on how warm your kitchen is.

Once the dough has risen, punch it down and knead for another minute before dividing into 6 (for regular) or 10 (for small) dough balls. Leave the balls to rise on a greased baking sheet loosely covered with plastic wrap. After around 30 minutes they should have puffed up again. In the meantime, preheat the oven to as hot as it will go, and pop in a large rimmed baking sheet to heat up.

Using your hands or a rolling pin, flatten out each dough ball and drizzle a little oil over both sides. Brush with some of the remaining honey, carefully lay on the heated baking sheet and place in the top part of the oven. After 5 minutes the naan should have puffed up and turned golden brown, a sign that it's ready. Eat hot, brushed with a little melted butter or ghee if you want to be indulgent.

SERVES 4
Prep time 5 minutes
Cook time 5 minutes

7–8 cups mustard greens, cut into large bite-size pieces
1 tbsp oil—I like canola oil or light olive oil
1 tbsp butter
2 tsp black mustard seeds

2 scallions, finely sliced
1 fresh red chile, seeded and finely sliced
2 garlic cloves, finely sliced
good pinch of sea salt and pepper

Wilted mustard greens (pictured)

I love greens. This recipe has become a firm favorite, as the flavors liven up even the most boring vegetables. I particularly like the deep earthiness of mustard greens, but you can use any greens you like. The central core in some of the outer leaves can be rather woody, so just cut it out.

Blanch the mustard greens by cooking them in a large saucepan of boiling water for a few minutes. Then drain and run them under cold water to keep their color. Drain well again.

Gently heat the oil and butter in a large skillet and stir in the remaining ingredients. Once the mustard seeds start to sizzle, add the mustard greens and cook for a few minutes until steaming and wilted.

SERVES 4
Prep time 5 minutes
Cook time 25 minutes

1 celery root, about 1 3/4 lb
2 3/4–3 cups milk, or just enough to cover when boiling
good pinch of saffron threads
4 green cardamom pods, bruised with a pestle and mortar

4 black peppercorns
2 Indian bay leaves
a few woody thyme sprigs
sea salt (optional)

Saffron, cardamom & thyme celery root

Celery root is one of the unsung heroes of the vegetable family. It is understated, underrated and underused! I love celery root for its nutty and aromatic flavor, which resembles celery but isn't quite as harsh. You can use celery root in many different ways, raw or cooked, and it always tastes delicious.

Prepare the celery root by trimming off the base that contains all the knots and cutting off the hard greenish skin. Roughly chop the rest and put in a saucepan. Pour over the milk so that the celery root is fully immersed and add the remaining ingredients. Bring to a gentle boil and cook for around 20 minutes until soft and tender.

Strain off the milk and discard the cardamom husks, bay leaves and thyme. Use a fork to mash the celery root until smooth, or you can use an immersion blender if you have one. Taste and add a little salt if you like. Serve as a great alternative to potatoes.

SERVES **4** AS A SNACK
Prep time 10 minutes
Cook time 2 minutes

¹/₂ tsp kalonji (black onion or
    nigella) seeds
¹/₂ tsp cumin seeds
¹/₂ tsp fennel seeds
2 crisp green apples,
    such as Granny Smith
grated zest and juice of
    1 lemon, or to taste

good pinch of sugar, or to taste
pinch of sea salt, or to taste
1¹/₄ cups plain Greek yogurt—
    you can use low-fat if you like
2 tbsp roughly chopped mint

Green apple relish

*There's something about green
apples that cleanses your palate
instantly. I remember making
this recipe a few years ago when
I needed something refreshing
yet cooling to have with some
spicy pork chops. I didn't have
any cucumbers rolling around
in my fridge, so I looked to the
fruit bowl and saw a shiny
green apple looking back at me.
I added a few pickling spices and
this relish has since become one
of my favorite dips to have
with almost anything.*

Lightly toast the spices in a heavy-bottomed skillet over a gentle
heat for a few minutes until fragrant and turning a light golden
brown. Pour them into a mortar ready for crushing with a pestle
once they have cooled a little.

In the meantime, grate the apples, with the skin, on a Microplane or
cheese grater, making sure you don't grate into the bitter core and
seeds. Add the lemon zest and squeeze over the lemon juice to stop
the apple coloring, then add a good pinch of sugar and salt before
stirring through the yogurt and mint.

Roughly crush the toasted spices and add to the relish. Taste and
adjust the seasoning with salt, sugar and lemon juice if you need to.

· MY SECRET ·
This relish works well
as a slaw base—just add
some shredded crunchy
purple cabbage and a few
finely chopped scallions,
and serve with
grilled meats.

SERVES 4 AS A SNACK
Prep time 10 minutes

30 cherry tomatoes (any color), seeds removed and roughly chopped
1 scallion, roughly chopped
1–2 fresh Indian finger chiles or jalapeños, seeds removed and finely chopped
1 tsp peeled and finely chopped fresh ginger

1 tbsp roughly chopped cilantro
good pinch of sugar, or to taste
good pinch of sea salt, or to taste
good pinch of cracked black peppercorns

Chunky tomato relish

This recipe is a version of a tomato salsa with a little background heat. It's perfect to have with poppadums, crisps or bread. If you like your dips fiery, then keep the seeds in the chile.

Mix all the ingredients together in a bowl, then taste and add more sugar or salt, depending on how you like it.

SERVES 4 AS A SNACK
Prep time 10 minutes, plus soaking

1 chipotle chile, soaked in warm water for 5 minutes
2 ripe avocados
juice of $1/2$ lime
1 scallion, finely chopped
4 cherry tomatoes, cut in half

$1/4$ tsp smoked paprika
good pinch of sea salt, or to taste
1 tbsp roughly chopped mint
1 tbsp roughly chopped cilantro

Fiery avo relish

I discovered smoked paprika a few years ago and I've been hooked ever since. I also love the flavor of chipotle chile, which is a smoked jalapeño, as it really fires dishes up. It tastes sensational in this relish, but if you don't have any, you can just add a regular chile. Try serving this with my Blazing Burgers (see page 114).

Drain the chipotle chile, then roughly chop.

Halve the avocados, remove the pits and peel, then smash the flesh with the back of a fork. Squeeze over the lime juice and then mix with the remaining ingredients. Taste and adjust the seasoning if you think it needs it. Serve immediately.

Chunky Tomato Relish

Green Apple Relish

Chile Jam

Sticky Sweet Date Chutney

Caramelized Onion
& Balsamic Chutney

Fiery Avo Relish

Mango Chutney

Cucumber Raita

Preserved Lemon & Garlic Pickle

SERVES 4
Prep time 5 minutes
Cook time 2 minutes

1 tsp cumin seeds (optional)
1 cucumber
1¼ cups plain Greek yogurt—
   you can use low-fat if you like
2 tbsp roughly chopped mint
   or cilantro

juice of ½ lemon
pinch of sugar, or to taste
pinch of sea salt, or to taste

Cucumber raita

I think this recipe needs little introduction. Cucumber raita is always eaten to cool down any chile heat, but sometimes I like to spice it up and throw in a chile or two. There are plenty of ways to gear up the flavor, so really play around with veggies, fruit and fresh herbs.

If using cumin seeds, lightly toast them in a heavy-bottomed skillet over a gentle heat for a few minutes until fragrant and turning a light golden brown. Pour them into a mortar ready for crushing with a pestle once they have cooled a little.

In the meantime, grate the cucumber, seeds and all, on a Microplane or cheese grater. Squeeze out any water before mixing with the yogurt, mint or cilantro and lemon juice. Season with a pinch of sugar and salt.

Roughly crush the toasted cumin seeds (if using) and add to the raita before tasting and adding more sugar and salt if you like.

Other ideas . . .
Why not layer up the spices in this dish by heating a few tablespoons of vegetable oil and frying off ½ teaspoon cumin seeds with 1 teaspoon black mustard seeds, a small handful of fresh, washed curry leaves and a dried red chile? Once the mixture is sizzling, simply pour it over the yogurt mixed with cucumber and season to taste with salt and pepper.

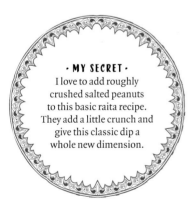

· MY SECRET ·
I love to add roughly crushed salted peanuts to this basic raita recipe. They add a little crunch and give this classic dip a whole new dimension.

MAKES ABOUT 1²/₃ LB
OR 1 JAR
Prep time 20 minutes,
plus maturing
Cook time 45 minutes

4 large soft ripe mangos, about
   2¹/₂ lb once you've peeled and
   pitted them, chopped into small
   bite-size pieces
3¹/₂ cups light brown sugar
1 cinnamon stick
1 tsp kalonji (black onion or
   nigella) seeds (optional)

3 dried red chiles, ripped so
   that the seeds can fall out
2 tbsp peeled and julienned
   fresh ginger
2¹/₃ cups distilled malt vinegar
²/₃ cup bourbon
good pinch of salt

Mango chutney

*This popular chutney has
made my family famous all
over the world. This is my
version of the recipe with the
addition of bourbon. It doesn't
overpower the chutney, but
rather adds some depth and
warmth. You can leave the
bourbon out if you wish—
just add more vinegar instead,
but make sure it's distilled
malt vinegar, as regular malt
vinegar is just too strong.*

Mix all the ingredients together in a heavy-bottomed saucepan and
boil for 40 to 45 minutes. It should thicken and be quite syrupy.

Pour into a sterilized (*see* My Secret, page 161) canning jar while hot.
Seal the jar, allow to cool completely, then move to a cool place and
leave for a week. This will give it time to mature. It should keep for
around 3 months.

· MY SECRET ·
Mango chutney is really
versatile. Add a heaped tablespoon
to plain Greek yogurt for a refreshing
dip, use in place of your usual
tomato-based pizza sauce topping
(see my naaza recipes on page 57)
or spread some on a cheese
sandwich—you won't
be disappointed!

MAKES ABOUT 2¹/₄ LB
OR 1 JAR
Prep time 5 minutes
Cook time around 30 minutes

2 tsp cumin seeds
5 dried red chiles or 1 tsp crushed
    red pepper flakes, depending
    on how hot you like it
3¹/₄ cups water

14 oz tamarind paste
2 cups light brown sugar
2²/₃ cups pitted dates, roughly
    chopped
good pinch of sea salt, or to taste

Sticky sweet date chutney

A good chutney should be sweet with a little hint of sourness. This recipe uses tamarind to add a wonderful sweet yet sour flavor to the already sticky sweet dates.

Lightly toast the cumin seeds and chiles or red pepper flakes in a heavy-bottomed saucepan over a gentle heat for a few minutes until fragrant and the seeds are turning a light golden brown.

Pour in the water before adding the tamarind, sugar and dates. Stir well and allow to simmer until the mixture has thickened. This will take 20 to 25 minutes, depending on the size of your pan. Turn off the heat and stir in a good pinch of salt.

Allow to cool until cool enough to taste and adjust the seasoning. Pour into a hot sterilized (*see* My Secret, page 161) canning jar. Seal the jar and keep in a cool place for up to 3 months.

· MY SECRET ·
This recipe tastes wonderful with smoked salt. Add a little less than regular sea salt, as it is very strong.

MAKES ABOUT 2¹/₄ LB
OR 1 QUART JAR
Prep time 10 minutes, plus
preserving and maturing
Cook time 15 minutes

2 tsp coriander seeds
1 tsp fennel seeds
3 Indian bay leaves
3 dried red chiles
¹/₃ cup plus 1 tbsp sea salt
6 unwaxed lemons
5 tbsp vegetable oil

2 tsp black mustard seeds
2 whole garlic heads, cloves
    separated, peeled and sliced
2¹/₄ cups white wine vinegar
1 cup plus 1–2 tbsp sugar
1–2 tsp chile powder

Preserved lemon & garlic pickle

Preserved lemons and garlic pickle are both well-known favorites and taste wonderful, but one day I had a thought— why not combine them and make a pickle that has the best of both? After testing a few versions, I created this amazing recipe that I'm sure you will absolutely love.

Lightly toast the coriander and fennel seeds, bay leaves and chiles in a heavy-bottomed skillet over a gentle heat for a few minutes until fragrant and the seeds are turning a light golden brown. Mix in the sea salt.

Cut the lemons into quarters, but not all the way through so that they are held together at the base. Tightly pack the salt mixture into the lemons and squeeze into a large ¹/₂ gallon clip-top canning jar. Fill the jar with water all the way to the top before sealing closed and leaving to preserve for around a month. Try to be patient and don't open the lid!

When the month is up, strain the salty liquid, keeping the spices and around ¹/₃ cup of the liquid. Wash the lemons under cold running water to remove all the salt and discard any flesh including all the white pith from the inside, leaving only the skin behind. Shred the skin into large slivers.

· MY SECRET ·
If you want your pickle to have an authentic Indian slant, use mustard oil instead of vegetable oil.

Gently heat the oil in a saucepan with the mustard seeds and the garlic. When the mustard seeds start to sizzle, toss in the slivers of preserved lemon, the vinegar, sugar, chile powder and reserved salty liquid with the drained spices. Boil for 5 to 10 minutes, or until the liquid has reduced by half.

Pour into a hot sterilized (*see* My Secret, page 161) quart canning jar. Seal the jar, allow to cool completely, then move to a cool place and allow to mature for a week. Once opened, this pickle will keep for 3 months.

Kitchen shortcuts

Everyone has their own cooking shortcuts: their kitchen secrets to make cooking a breeze. I love opening up my fridge and pantry to discover concoctions and potions I've made that were developed in the hope they would help me in some way. I grew up with a pantry full of shortcuts. There were garam masalas everywhere; some were dry and the rest were wet. Spice pastes are a dream for any cook: see pages 134–35 for some of my faves.

When my grandfather invented spice pastes it wasn't because people didn't have time to cook, it was purely because British cooks didn't know how to cook well with spices. Times have changed and spice pastes have become a pantry favorite for even the best cooks as it's easier to grab a jar of paste when you're in a rush, than it is to make your own garam masala, especially seeing as spices taste fresher locked in oil than sitting dry in a pantry. As well as a pantry full of pastes, I always make sure I have some of my own kitchen secrets that I go to time and time again when I need that personal touch.

SCENTED OIL
I love keeping some spiced oils not only for cooking, but also for dipping warm bread into. Some of my favorite flavor combos are listed here:

Chile & garlic oil
2 fresh red chiles (slit down the middle)
4 large garlic cloves (bashed to release their flavor)
1 sprig of rosemary
1¼ cups olive oil

Black mustard & dried red chile oil
2 teaspoons black mustard seeds
5 dried red chiles (ripped in half)
⅓ cup plus 1 tbsp mustard oil and 1 scant cup canola oil, or 1¼ cups canola oil

Rosemary & black pepper oil
3 sprigs of rosemary
2 teaspoons whole black peppercorns
1¼ cups olive oil

Turmeric & ginger oil
2-inch piece fresh turmeric root, peeled and thinly sliced (or 1 teaspoon ground turmeric)
2-inch piece fresh ginger, peeled and thinly sliced
1¼ cups canola oil

For each oil, gently heat all ingredients in a large saucepan for 5 minutes. Do not boil. Remove from the heat, allow to cool and transfer to an airtight bottle. Store in a cool, dark place.

TADKAS

A wonderful way to add flavor to lentils and veggies is to infuse spices in a little oil and pour the oil over the top. You will get a flavor hit with each bite and it's a popular cooking technique in India. Unlike the scented oils that you can keep, tadkas are made at the last minute—have a look at my Tadka Dhal recipe on page 154 for some inspiration of what spices you can use: think aromatics and seeds rather than ground powders. You need to release the aromas and flavor from the spices so gently heat them for a few minutes before turning off the heat. If they burn they will taste very bitter.

READY-MADE MASALAS

Having a few spice blends at the ready is a great way to save time in the kitchen.

Coriander & cumin flavor base

4 tablespoons cumin seeds
2 tablespoons coriander seeds

A simple masala used by most Indian cooks. Simply grind the seeds together, then store in an airtight container in a cool, dark place.

Chai masala

I love chai (Indian tea) and always make up enough chai masala to last me a few weeks. See my recipe for Heart-Warming Chai on page 213 for what spices I grind.

Toasted cumin

Lightly toast whole cumin seeds in a dry skillet for a few minutes; keep them moving to stop them from burning. When they are golden brown and you can smell the aromas, remove from the heat. Allow to cool before grinding as coarse as you like it. Store in an airtight container in a cool, dark place.

Chaat masala

Easy to make, but you can easily buy this well-loved masala from your Asian store. As much as I have harped on about making your masalas fresh, this is one you could buy and not feel bad about. Its tangy, sour and salty flavor— full of fruity, sour dried mango powder, black salt, cumin, asafetida, coriander and hints of chile—will add a je ne sais quoi to your dish. Once you've tried it you will be hooked and want to sprinkle it on everything.

CHAPTER

7

SUGAR & SPICE

MAKES 8 MINIS
OR 1 LARGE
(SERVES 6 TO 8)
Prep time 10 minutes
Cook time 30 minutes

¾ cup plus 2 tbsp sugar
¼ tsp ground cinnamon
8 green cardamom pods, bruised
   with a pestle and mortar
3½ oz (7 tablespoons) unsalted
   butter, chilled and cut into cubes,
   plus extra for greasing

3 Granny Smith apples, peeled,
   cored, cut into ½-inch-thick
   wedges and rubbed with the juice
   of ½ lemon to stop them from
   browning
10½ oz store-bought puff pastry,
   rolled out to ⅛ inch thick
freshly grated nutmeg, for sprinkling
whipped cream or ice cream, for
   serving

Baby apple tarte tatin with spiced caramel

Apple tarte tatin is on my foodie bucket list; it tops my short list of best dishes of all time. A year ago a friend of mine set up a supper club where you submit the recipes you would like to have at your last supper. If your menu were to be picked, a supper club would be held in your honor featuring your ultimate menu. Without hesitation this recipe sprang to mind and it will always remain a firm favorite. The most outstanding example I've ever tried was at a Michelin-starred Galvin restaurant in London. I return time after time just for the escargots and the tarte tatin and I can't help but smile every time I visit, as I know what delights are in store for me.

I am using store-bought puff pastry for this recipe, as it's easier, but feel free to make your own if you like.

Preheat the oven to 400°F.

Make the caramel by gently heating the sugar with the cinnamon and cardamom in a large skillet until it melts. (If you are making a large tarte tatin, make sure your skillet is ovenproof.)

This bit is important. As the sugar melts, it will start to turn golden brown, but don't let it turn too dark or your caramel will be bitter. As soon as it's ready, turn down the heat and carefully beat in the chilled cubed butter. Place the apple wedges in the pan.

Generously grease 8 holes of a muffin (or cupcake) tray with butter. Use a cutter slightly larger than the size of the tray holes to cut out 8 disks from the puff pastry. Prick each pastry disk a few times with a fork. This will stop it puffing up too much in the oven.

Once the apple wedges have been steeping in the caramel for a few minutes, turn off the heat. Carefully spoon the steeped apple wedges into the tray holes, being generous with the caramel but making sure to reserve some for drizzling over later, and then sprinkle over the nutmeg. Top each hole with a pastry disk and tuck in the sides so that the apples are covered and snug in the tin.

Bake for 20 minutes, or until the pastry is golden brown. Remove from the oven and allow to cool for a few minutes before inverting a plate over the tray and turning it all upside down to release the tartes. (You may need to tap the base of the tray to help them out.) The pastry should be at the bottom with the sticky, spiced, caramelized apples on top.

Spoon over the reserved caramel and serve with a good dollop of whipped cream or ice cream. It's heavenly!

SERVES 12
Prep time 15 minutes,
plus freezing

4 eggs
¹/₄ cup plus 2 tsp superfine sugar
2 tsp ground green cardamom
2¹/₄ cups heavy whipping cream
³/₄ cup roasted hazelnuts, ground,
   plus an extra 2 tbsp chopped
³/₄ cup Nutella hazelnut chocolate
   spread

Roast hazelnut & cardamom ice cream

This recipe features three of my favorite ingredients: roast hazelnuts, Nutella hazelnut chocolate spread and the sweet spice cardamom. The ice cream is rather indulgent, as it uses heavy whipping cream to set it—wonderful if you don't have an ice-cream maker. I love having extra in the freezer as a sweet treat, which is why this recipe is enough for 12 servings.

· MY SECRET ·
This tastes great with hot
chocolate sauce. Try adding
a tablespoon of peanut
butter to melting chocolate
for some extra nuttiness.

Get 3 large bowls. Separate the eggs and put the yolks in one bowl and the whites in another, making sure this bowl is particularly squeaky clean (*see page 196*). Add the sugar and cardamom to the yolks, then pour the cream into the third bowl.

Whisk up the whites, preferably using an electric whisk, until stiff peaks forms. This means when you lift the whisk out the whites will stand up and stay up.

Whisk the egg yolks, using a clean electric whisk, until light and pale in color.

Finally, whisk the cream, using a clean electric whisk, until it just holds its shape (soft peaks).

Fold the ground hazelnuts into the cream before mixing it into the beaten yolks. Then gently fold in the whites, trying not to knock the air out of them. Stir through the Nutella—I like to swirl it through instead of completely mixing it in. Pour it all into a freezer-proof container, sprinkle over the chopped roasted hazelnuts and pop in the freezer, ideally overnight.

MAKES AROUND
30 MINI MUFFINS
OR 8 LARGE ONES
Prep time 10 minutes
Cook time 15–20 minutes

3/4 cup plus 2 tbsp all-purpose flour
2 tsp baking powder
1/2 tsp baking soda
2 tsp ground cinnamon
1/2 cup dark brown sugar
pinch of sea salt
5 tbsp unsalted butter, melted and
  cooled, plus extra, if not using
  paper cases, for greasing

1/3 cup plus 1 tbsp milk
1/3 cup plus 1 tbsp buttermilk
1 large egg, whisked

Maple cream
1/3 cup plus 1 tbsp heavy whipping
  cream
3 tbsp maple syrup

Cinnamon mini muffins with maple cream

Muffins are great at any time of the day and they are so simple to make it amazes me that anyone would buy them. I have used buttermilk as well as milk in this recipe, but you can opt for one or the other if you prefer—just make sure you use 2/3 cup plus 2 tbsp of whichever you choose.

Preheat the oven to 400°F and either line 30 holes of mini muffin trays with mini paper cases or grease really well with butter. (Or line 8 holes of a regular-size muffin tray.)

Sift the flour, baking powder, baking soda and cinnamon together into a bowl. Stir through the sugar and salt, making sure you break up any lumps.

In another bowl, whisk the melted butter, milks and egg together.

Make a well in the center of the dry mixture and pour in the wet mixture. Fold them together, making sure you don't overmix the batter. Lumps make a lighter muffin!

Fill the paper cases or greased holes with heaped teaspoonfuls of the batter and bake for 15 to 20 minutes. The muffins should be springy to the touch and an inserted skewer should come out clean when they are cooked.

>>>

· MY SECRET ·
These are perfect to make ahead if you are short on time. Mix the dry ingredients in one bowl and whisk the wet ingredients in another. Pop the wet mix in the fridge. When you are ready, all you have to do is pour the wet mix into the dry, fill your muffin cases and you're ready to bake.

Remove from the tin and leave to cool slightly on a wire rack. In the meantime, make the maple cream by simply whisking the cream with the maple syrup until it forms soft peaks. Serve the muffins next to a generously filled pot of the maple cream.

Other ideas . . .
I use this recipe as a base for other wonderful flavors, one of my favorites being Pecan Muffins with Saffron Cream.

Pecan muffins with saffron cream

Stir ²/₃ cup to ³/₄ cup roughly chopped pecans through the dry muffin mixture before mixing in the wet ingredients. Then soak a really good pinch of saffron threads in 1 tablespoon warm milk for a few minutes before whisking it with the cream and maple syrup.

Cinnamon raisin muffins with cardamom cream

Gently heat ²/₃ cup to ³/₄ cup raisins with enough orange juice to cover in a small saucepan until the raisins are plump. Strain off the juice and add the raisins to the wet muffin mixture. Follow the steps for the cinnamon muffin recipe but add ¹/₂ teaspoon of crushed green cardamom seeds to the maple cream.

Carrot & ginger muffins with maple cream

Add 2 large grated carrots to the dry muffin mix and swap the ground cinnamon for ground ginger. I also love to use all buttermilk for this recipe. Add some orange zest to the cream and whip up with the maple syrup.

SERVES 6 TO 8
Prep time 15 minutes,
plus chilling
Cook time 3 minutes

3¹/₂ tbs unsalted butter
7 oz ginger snaps, or use digestive
biscuits with 1 tsp ground ginger
3 chunks of stem ginger in syrup,
including some of the syrup from
the jar
10¹/₂ oz cream cheese—I like
Philadelphia

5¹/₂ oz creamed coconut—the ones
in blocks or packets
1 cup plus 2 tbsp heavy whipping
cream
grated zest and juice of 1 lime
(see My Secret, below)
¹/₂ cup coconut flakes or dried
unsweetened coconut, toasted
(see My Secret, page 182)

Coconut & ginger cheesecake

*I love cheesecakes and have
never been a fan of the New
York–style ones that are baked.
I much prefer the chilled ones,
so here is a recipe that is great
to make ahead and keep
chilled in the fridge until you
need it. Make sure you buy
creamed coconut, available
in blocks or in individual
sachets, and not coconut
cream, as the latter contains
too much coconut water and
your cheesecake won't set. I've
used a springform cake pan
with a removable bottom,
which you shouldn't need
to grease with butter if it's
nonstick, but you can easily
prepare these individually in
pretty glasses.*

Gently melt the butter in a saucepan, then pour into a food
processor with the ginger biscuits and stem ginger. Blitz until
combined. Tightly press the crumbs into the base of a 7-inch round
springform pan with a removable bottom and spread out so that it's
an even thickness all over. Pop in the fridge to chill and set while you
make the cheesecake filling.

Beat together the cream cheese, creamed coconut, heavy whipping
cream, lime juice and around 3 tablespoons of the stem ginger
syrup, or more if you like it sweet. (If you happen to be using
crystallized ginger instead and don't have any syrup, add some
confectioners' sugar to taste.) Spread on top of the ginger crumb
base and put back in the fridge to set for a few hours.

When you are ready to serve, sprinkle the cheesecake all over with
the toasted coconut and the lime zest.

· MY SECRET ·
I like to make speedy candied
peel for sprinkling on top of the
cheesecake. Cut pared lime zest into
strips, remove any white pith and heat in
simple syrup for around 10 minutes.
Carefully (because they will be very hot)
strain the strips, roll them in superfine
sugar and allow to cool and crisp up.
Store any extra in an airtight
container for other sweet treats.

MAKES 16 TRUFFLES
Prep time 5 minutes, plus
chilling and warming
Cook time 10 minutes

3¹/₂ oz dark chocolate, chopped into
  small pieces
¹/₃ cup plus 1 tbsp heavy whipping
  cream
3¹/₂ tbsp unsalted butter
pinch of sea salt

Flavorings
dash of orange juice or liqueur, such
  as Amaretto or Tia Maria; a pinch
  of chile powder (these are optional
  and you needn't stick to only these;
  the sky's the limit!)

Stuffings
nuts; raisins; finely chopped candied
  ginger—goes well with a cocoa
  powder coating

Coatings
finely chopped nuts, such as
  pistachios, hazelnuts or almonds;
  dried unsweetened coconut,
  toasted (*see* My Secret, below) or
  flavored with ground cinnamon or
  grated orange rind; cocoa powder

Decadent chocolate truffles

Bringing out a plate of homemade chocolate truffles at the end of a meal always gets the "mmmmm" factor. This is a simple base recipe to use and I'm sharing with you some of my favorite ingredients that I like to add to spruce them up. Use good-quality dark chocolate with at least 70% cocoa solids. You can always mix in a bit of milk chocolate if dark isn't your thing.

Pour boiling water into a saucepan so that it comes a third of the way up the sides of the pan. Pop a heatproof bowl on top, making sure the base of it doesn't touch the water, and tip in the chocolate. Stir it every now and again while it's melting.

In the meantime, gently heat the cream with the butter in another saucepan until the butter has melted. Don't let the cream boil.

Once the chocolate has melted, remove the bowl from the pan and pour in the cream mixture. Add the salt—trust me, it brings out even more flavor in the chocolate—and stir well until the chocolate is glossy. At this point you can stir in some flavorings, such as orange juice, a liqueur or even a pinch of chile powder. Pop in the fridge to chill and set for at least 2 hours.

Once set, take the truffle mix out of the fridge and allow to warm up for a few minutes while you get the rest of your flavorings ready. To make the truffles, simply scoop up a scant tablespoonful of the chocolate mix and quickly roll it in your hands—you have to be quick or it will melt. Stuff the truffles if you like and/or roll them in your chosen coating.

Lay the truffles on a rimmed baking sheet lined with parchment paper and pop them in the fridge until you need them. They will keep for 3 days, if they last that long!

· MY SECRET ·
It's easy to toast coconut.
Heat dried unsweetened
coconut gently in a dry skillet,
moving it around often, until
light golden brown. Toasting
coconut releases its lovely
nutty flavor.

SERVES 4
Prep time 5 minutes
Cook time 8 minutes

3/4 cup sugar
grated zest and juice of 2 lemons
1 vanilla pod
5 green cardamom pods
2 star anise
2 cinnamon sticks
4 peaches, cut in half and pits removed
1 1/4 cups blueberries
1 1/4 cups blackberries

Saffron crème
4 heaped tbsp crème fraîche or plain Greek yogurt
good pinch of saffron threads, soaked in 1 tbsp warm water or warm milk for a few minutes

Aromatic steeped fruit with saffron crème

This is a recipe for fuss-free days when you fancy something sweet with little effort. By making a simple sugar syrup, you can poach your fruit in minutes. I've chosen peaches, blueberries and blackberries purely because their fantastic colors permeate the syrup, turning it deep crimson, but any soft fruit works here. Serving it with a saffron crème makes this dessert extra special.

Gently heat the sugar and lemon zest and juice in a large skillet. Split the vanilla pod down the middle lengthwise and run the back of the knife down the inside to release the seeds. Add them to the pan with the pod. Bash the cardamoms with a pestle and mortar to release the seeds and then add them all to the sugar mixture with the star anise and cinnamon sticks.

Lay the peaches, cut-side down, in the syrup and toss in the berries. Cook the fruit for 5 minutes, basting with the syrup, before flipping the peaches over and turning off the heat.

Make the saffron crème by mixing the crème fraîche or yogurt with the saffron and its soaking liquid. Serve the aromatic steeped fruit with a good dollop of the saffron crème.

SERVES 8
Prep time 10 minutes,
plus chilling

1¹/₄ cups full-fat plain Greek yogurt
7 oz ricotta cheese
1 tsp ground cinnamon
³/₄ cup plus 2 tbsp pomegranate juice
3 tbsp pomegranate molasses
4–5 tbsp grenadine or honey, to taste
    (optional)
seeds of 1 pomegranate, to decorate

Pomegranate & ricotta frozen yogurt

Frozen yogurt has to be one of the best recipes invented. I also just love the combination of pomegranate and yogurt— and here I'm using both pomegranate molasses and pomegranate juice. You can buy pomegranate molasses in most supermarkets, but if you can't find it, then simply leave it out. The color of this frozen yogurt is stunning if you add grenadine, a syrup that was originally made from pomegranates, although nowadays other berries are added. It doesn't matter which one you use as long as it's free from artificial colors.

Using a blender or food processor, whizz the yogurt and ricotta together until smooth. Toss in the cinnamon, pomegranate juice and pomegranate molasses and mix well. If using, add the grenadine a tablespoon at a time until the mixture is vibrant pink. If you aren't using grenadine, then you may want to add some honey to make the yogurt sweeter. Remember that some of the sweetness will be lost once it's frozen.

Pour the mixture into a freezer-proof container and freeze for about 2 hours until almost frozen. Then whizz it up again in your blender or food processor, or use an immersion blender if you have one, to break up any ice crystals that will have formed. Return the mixture to the freezer. Do this at least 3 times, at 2-hour intervals, to remove any ice crystals. Then freeze for a few hours more to really firm up.

When ready to serve, leave the frozen yogurt out of the freezer for around 10 minutes before scooping and sprinkling with the pomegranate seeds.

· MY SECRET ·
Frozen yogurt is usually made with yogurt alone, but by adding ricotta, it freezes much better, as yogurt forms a lot of ice crystals unless you use an ice-cream maker. So my recipe doesn't need an ice-cream maker and is a breeze to prepare!

Mum and me at our first home in
Newton-le-Willows, Wigan. Partners
in crime from the word go!

A mini me, of course!

Baa at Nayan's wedding.

One of our classic family holiday shots from a
Caribbean cruise (my parents loved cruising!). Me
looking good as gold (front right) with my brothers
Neeraj (front center) and Nayan (front left); Mum
and Dad (back left); and Bapuji and Baa (back right).

When Mum and I (left) started working together we realized how much we had in common. She loved passing the baton (or in our case the rolling pin!) on to me and we wrote a cookbook together to celebrate fifty years of Patak's. Getting to work and learn with my mum will be something I remember forever.

Dad and I are often in the kitchen together at family get-togethers cooking up a storm.

A classic Christmas sight (above): Mum taste-testing the sauce for Dad's ribs. Dad loves making his special ribs for us at Christmas (as much as we love eating them—they are soooooo good). That he is a vegetarian makes us appreciate them even more.

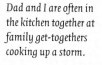

Me and my fabulous Leiths girlies (left to right: Beata, Amparo, Mel, and Laura). Wine and cheese nights are one of our favorite ways to catch up. This was my turn to host at my apartment in London.

Me on a promo shoot. I am so happy and proud to be part of Baa and Bapuji's continuing legacy while forging a food route of my own.

SERVES 4
Prep time 10 minutes
Cook time 10 minutes

6 ripe peaches, plums and
nectarines (or any stone fruit),
cut in half and pits removed
8 green cardamom pods
4 cloves
1/2 tsp ground cinnamon
2 tbsp raisins
2 tbsp honey, plus extra (optional)
for drizzling

Pistachio cream
6 tbsp plain Greek yogurt, or heavy
whipping cream if you want to add
some indulgence
1/4 cup shelled pistachio nuts,
roughly chopped
grated zest of 1 lemon

Roast stone fruit & honey with pistachio cream

As a lover of desserts, I'm always looking for quick sugar fixes, which is why I came up with this recipe. I love having friends over for dinner and so I created this fuss-free dish to make my prep easier. It takes just minutes to put together and then all you need to do is pop it in the oven for 10 minutes. It's that simple!

· MY SECRET ·
I love to sprinkle over
some crushed ginger
biscuits just before serving
to add some extra crunch.
It's not sophisticated but
it tastes great!

Preheat the oven to 350°F and line a rimmed baking sheet with foil.

Lay the stone fruit, cut-side up, on the lined baking sheet. Bash the cardamom pods and cloves together with a pestle and mortar to release their aromatic flavors. You can discard the cardamom husks if you like, but I prefer to leave mine in. Sprinkle over the stone fruit with the cinnamon. Add some raisins to the hollows where the pits were and drizzle over the 2 tablespoons of honey.

Roast for 10 minutes, or until the flesh of the fruit has softened. But don't leave them in too long, as they can quickly collapse and go mushy.

In the meantime, make the pistachio cream by mixing the yogurt or cream with most of the pistachios and most of the lemon zest. Taste and add a little honey if you need to, remembering that the stone fruit is naturally sweet—you can always drizzle it over at the end if you aren't sure.

Allow the roast fruit to cool a little. Spoon over a good dollop of pistachio cream and serve sprinkled with the remaining pistachios and lemon zest, drizzled with a little extra honey if you like.

SERVES 6 TO 8
Prep time 15 minutes
Cook time 1¹/₂ hours,
plus cooling

2 egg whites
¹/₂ cup superfine sugar
2 tsp strong coffee—simply
   mix 2 tsp coffee granules
   with 1 tbsp boiling water

Spiced cream
³/₄ cup heavy whipping cream
¹/₂ tsp ground cinnamon
good pinch of ground
   green cardamom
pinch of freshly grated
   nutmeg (optional)

grated chocolate, to decorate

Spiced latte meringue

When I was training to be a chef we had special creative days every now and again. After learning all about the different types of meringue (and there are quite a few methods), we were all asked to come up with an idea for a creative meringue day. Ever since then I've been hooked on meringues and I adore them. They are easy to make, but there are a few rules to follow to ensure that they work every time. Make sure all your equipment (bowls, whisk, spoons and so on) is scrupulously clean—the whites won't whisk up properly if they aren't. Use room-temperature eggs and, lastly, do please allow the meringues to cool completely before diving in.

   This is one of my favorite recipes, using rich coffee and sweet spices. Making a simple coffee meringue means you can add any of your favorite spices to the cream topping. Every mouthful screams Spiced Latte.

Preheat the oven to 250°F and line a large rimmed baking sheet with parchment paper.

Whisk up the egg whites in a very clean large bowl until you get stiff peaks and they have quadrupled in volume. I find it easier to do this with an electric whisk. Keep whisking and add the sugar 1 tablespoon at a time. The whites will turn glossy and shiny. Fold in the coffee—I like to lightly fold it in to create a marbled effect.

Pour the meringue into the middle of the lined baking sheet and spread it evenly into a circle. Don't worry if there are peaks on top and it's not completely smooth, as that's half the charm of meringues. Bake for 1¹/₂ hours. You will know it's cooked as the paper will come away easily from the base and the meringue will be dry. Allow to cool while you make the spiced cream.

Place the cream in a large bowl and sprinkle in the spices. Whip up until it just holds its shape (soft peaks). Keep the cream chilled until you need it.

Once the meringue has completely cooled, top with the spiced cream and sprinkle over some grated chocolate to decorate.

· MY SECRET ·
To make individual meringues, dollop even-size amounts of the meringue mixture onto the lined baking sheet, then flatten them a little. Bake for about an hour, depending on the size and depth of your meringues.

CHAPTER 8

COCKTAIL TIME

SERVES 4
Prep time 5 minutes

2¹/₃ cups plain Greek yogurt—you can use low-fat if you prefer
2¹/₃ cups chilled water, or have a few ice cubes at the ready
really good pinch of sea salt (for salty lassi) or sugar (for sweet lassi), or to taste

good pinch of toasted cumin seeds (*see* page 171), roughly crushed with a pestle and mortar, or to taste, plus extra to serve

Creamy, salty & sweet lassi

Lassi is the cooling yogurt drink served with many Indian meals. The best lassi I ever had was on the streets of Amritsar in Punjab, which is famous for this rich and creamy drink. Using the traditional old-fashioned tools, they freshly churn homemade curd until frothy, before pouring it from a height into tall glasses. It's then topped with a huge scoop of fresh cream from the top of the curd, making it a meal in itself— luxuriously rich and too yummy for words.

You can find both salty and sweet lassis, and I prefer the former. I grew up with fresh lassi made with a masala (see recipe opposite)—sometimes just toasted cumin, other times even more special with whole cloves, fresh curry leaves and cilantro.

Whisk together the yogurt and water (and ice if you need it) until frothy and bubbly. Add the salt or sugar and toasted cumin and whisk again.

Taste and adjust the flavor with salt or sugar, if you need to, before pouring into 4 tall glasses. Sprinkle over a little more toasted cumin before serving.

· MY SECRET ·
Try adding a flavored salt such as lavender salt, fleur de sel or rock salt. It will add depth to the taste and in some cases a little color.

SERVES 4
Prep time 5 minutes

2¼ cups plain Greek yogurt—you can use low-fat if you prefer
2⅓ cups chilled water, or have a few ice cubes at the ready
6 tbsp prepared ripe fruit, such as mango pulp, mashed strawberries or pureed berries

good pinch of green cardamom seeds, crushed with a pestle and mortar, or ground cinnamon, plus extra to serve (optional)
pinch of sugar, to taste (optional)

Sweet fruity lassi

Sweet lassis are made using pureed fresh fruit with the occasional addition of sweet spices. In Pakistan they sometimes add saffron, which tastes divine.

Whisk together the yogurt and water (and ice if you need it) until frothy and bubbly. Stir in the fruit and whisk again.

Taste and adjust the flavor with the spices (if using) and sugar, if you need to. Pour into 4 tall glasses and sprinkle over a little more spice (if using) before serving.

SERVES 4
Prep time 5 minutes
Cook time 3 minutes

2⅓ cups plain Greek yogurt—you can use low-fat if you prefer
2⅓ cups chilled water, or have a few ice cubes at the ready
2 tbsp vegetable oil—you can use ghee (clarified butter) if you prefer
a few cloves

1 tsp cumin seeds
around 10 fresh curry leaves (*see* My Secret, page 20)
1 Indian finger chile or jalapeño, slit down the middle but left whole
sea salt
a few tbsp chopped cilantro

Salty masala lassi

To make a salty masala lassi like the one I grew up with, you need to temper some spices before pouring into the whisked yogurt.

Whisk together the yogurt and water (and ice if you need it) until frothy and bubbly.

Gently heat the oil (traditionally it would be made using ghee) in a heavy-bottomed skillet and add the spices, curry leaves and chile. Once they are sizzling, carefully pour into the frothy yogurt mix, including the chile, and add salt to taste.

Stir the cilantro through the lassi and pour into 4 tall glasses to serve.

6 tbsp pomegranate juice
small handful of pomegranate seeds
750ml bottle chilled Prosecco

Pomegranate bellini

Although bellinis are traditionally made with peach, I prefer to make mine with jewel-colored pomegranate.

Add 1 tablespoon pomegranate juice to each of your glasses and toss in a few pomegranate seeds.

Top up with chilled Prosecco.

4 tbsp blood orange juice
dash of orange blossom water
750ml bottle chilled Prosecco
strips of orange zest, to garnish (optional)

Orange blossom bellini

The combination of orange blossom and blood orange juice is incredible, and even better when mixed with Prosecco. You can find orange blossom water in the baking aisle of the supermarket, but go easy with it, as it's strong. This is a fantastic start to any meal.

Mix the orange juice with the orange blossom water and divide among 6 glasses.

Top up with chilled Prosecco and garnish with a twist of orange zest if you like.

· MY SECRET ·
If you want your bellinis dressed to impress, add a cinnamon stick to each glass before topping up with Prosecco.

OPPOSITE PAGE:
Left: Salty masala lassi
Center: Pomegranate bellini
Right: Orange blossom bellini

SERVES 4
Prep time 2 minutes

¹/₃ cup plus 1–2 tbsp bourbon
¹/₃ cup cold espresso or
  super-strong coffee
¹/₂ cup Kahlúa coffee liqueur
¹/₃ cup crème de cacao (optional)
a few ice cubes

To garnish
good pinch of ground cinnamon
coffee beans

Malabar espresso martini

The Malabar Coast on the southern part of the west shore of India brings back wonderful memories of fresh seafood and tantalizing spices of the south. Whenever I visit the area I feel somewhat spellbound, and I think it's solely down to the waving palm trees, incredible food and holiday surroundings. For that reason I've named this martini a Malabar martini and added smoky bourbon instead of vodka. It will make you feel magical and mysterious just like the Malabar Coast.

Pour the bourbon, coffee, Kahlúa and crème de cacao (if using) into a cocktail shaker. Add a few ice cubes and shake well until muddled together and frothy.

Strain into 4 glasses and sprinkle over a little cinnamon and a few coffee beans to garnish.

· MY SECRET ·
The harder you shake the drink, the more white froth you'll get, which will give this martini its signature white foamy top.

about 1 cup dark golden rum
1¼ cups coconut cream (the creamy
    top layer of a can of coconut milk
    will work)
1⅔ cups pineapple juice
lots of crushed ice
4 star anise, for muddling
    and garnishing

Pineapple anise colada

I was a cruise child. My family took me on lots of cruises when I was young because they are the ultimate stress-free holiday. You get on board and everything is taken care of for the entire trip, even childcare, as there are kids' clubs every day. I lost count of how many virgin piña coladas I had throughout those years, and as I grew older I started having the ones laced with dark rum. It tastes great with a little hint of exotic star anise, and the "stars" look ever so pretty, so make sure you top each glass with a little star before serving.

Add all the ingredients except 2 of the star anise to a cocktail shaker. Shake well until creamy and blended.

Remove the star anise, rinse with water and set aside.

Pour the colada into 4 glasses, with more crushed ice if you need it, and top each with a star anise.

SERVES 4
Prep time 2–5 minutes

1¼-inch piece fresh ginger, peeled
    and thickly sliced
2¼ cups cranberry juice
grated zest and juice of ½ lime
4 cinnamon sticks, to serve
lots of crushed ice
2⅓ cups chilled sparkling water

Crimson ginger sparkler

*This is an alcohol-free cocktail
full of fresh cranberry and lime
juice and warming ginger
and cinnamon.*

Bash the ginger slices with a pestle and mortar to release
some of their juice.

Mix the ginger with the cranberry juice, lime juice, cinnamon
sticks and some crushed ice to infuse the flavors. Strain if
you wish (reserving the cinnamon sticks) or pour directly
into 4 tumblers filled with more crushed ice.

Top up with the sparkling water and sprinkle over the lime
zest. Place a cinnamon stick in each glass and serve.

SERVES 4
Prep time 2–5 minutes

1 cup lychee juice
2 cups apple juice
good pinch of freshly grated nutmeg
lots of crushed ice
2 cups chilled sparkling water
apple slices, to garnish (optional)

Lychee, apple & nutmeg crush

*The flavors in this mocktail
scream dessert. Apples and
nutmeg are a match made in
heaven, and when you throw
lychees into the mix, you've got
yourself one amazing drink.*

Mix all the ingredients except the sparkling water in a pitcher.

Pour into 4 tumblers, top up with the sparkling water and
garnish with apple slices (if using).

OPPOSITE PAGE:
Left: Lychee, apple & nutmeg crush
Center: Malabar espresso martini
Right: Crimson ginger sparkler

1–2 tbsp maple syrup, or to taste
20 mint leaves, plus extra to garnish
1 cup your favorite rum
2 limes, cut into quarters
lots of crushed ice
2 cups soda water

Maple & lime mojito

This is a wonderful rum cocktail to make if you have a menu filled with spice. This recipe is full of refreshing lime flavor and sweet maple syrup, with a little cooling mint in the background.

Tip the maple syrup and mint leaves into a bowl or cocktail shaker and bash together until the leaves are broken and you can smell the fresh aroma of the mint. Add the rum and squeeze in the juice from the lime quarters. Toss in the lime quarters and a little crushed ice and mix together.

Fill 4 tumblers with more crushed ice and strain the mojito mix into the glasses. Top up with the soda water, taste and add a little more maple syrup if you like your mojitos sweet. Garnish with a few extra mint leaves.

S E R V E S 4
Prep time 5 minutes
Cook time 6 minutes

2¹/₃ cups water
4 tsp fresh tea leaves or 4 tea bags—
    I like Darjeeling but any will do
8 cloves
8 green cardamom pods
¹/₂ tsp fennel seeds

¹/₂ tsp black peppercorns
1 tsp peeled and grated fresh
    ginger
handful of mint leaves (optional)
2¹/₃ cups milk
sugar, to taste (optional)

Heart-warming chai

I fell in love with chai from the moment I tried its heavenly sweet flavor. Chai is ubiquitous in India, and each spice blend is slightly different. It's always full of flavor and usually overly sweet. I like to add sugar to taste, as the spices sweeten up the tea a little and so you may not even need to add any. Like most families, ours had our very own secret masala chai spice blend. The secret was always closely guarded and only ever passed down to a worthy recipient when the time was right. There are many good ready-made chai masalas you can buy, but there is really nothing like adding fresh spices to your bubbling tea leaves to create the perfect heart-warming chai.

Pour the water into a large saucepan, add the tea and turn the heat on. Gently crush the cloves, cardamoms, fennel seeds and peppercorns with a pestle and mortar. Stir into the pan with the ginger and mint (if using) and bring the water to a rolling boil.

Once the water is boiling, pour the milk into the tea and bring to a boil, then turn off the heat. Taste and add sugar if you like. Strain the tea and serve piping hot.

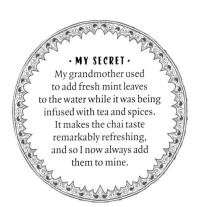

· MY SECRET ·
My grandmother used to add fresh mint leaves to the water while it was being infused with tea and spices. It makes the chai taste remarkably refreshing, and so I now always add them to mine.

Wine & spice

Choosing what to drink with spicy food can be a minefield. With this is mind, a few years ago I decided to take the gold standard of wine qualifications and studied the Wine and Spirit Education Trust advanced module in London. Two weeks full time at wine school sounds like a dream, but it was a lot harder than it sounds and although I tasted some incredible wines I soon learned that the world of wine is absolutely huge and always changing.

If you are like me and prefer to drink wine with an Indian meal, then it's useful to know what style of wine will complement your dish. I don't claim to be a wine expert, far from it, so think of this as a rough guide to different wine styles that have been found to work well with spice-infused recipes.

It's good to pick a wine that has a little sweetness and good acidity as most spice recipes have a hint of both. This could be from the tomatoes, lemons, added sugar and even the sweet nature of some spices. Try to avoid oak and high-alcohol wines, as this will accentuate the heat in the dish. I prefer red wines that are lighter in style as heavy tannic wines can make your food taste bitter, but do please your own palate. Wine is subjective and it's better to choose one you like rather than to drink one because someone said it works.

There is no one wine that fits all so think about what spices you are using, how much chile you've added, and how heavy the sauce is (if any). In some cuisines the protein is the star of the dish and the wine should match it accordingly, but with Asian food this isn't the case. If your protein is laced with spice or coated in sauce, you need something to balance these elements instead.

There are so many good wine styles, as well as excellent sparkling wines and champagnes, that match with spice-driven dishes, so don't be shy to experiment. Here are just a few of my favorites to help you on your way of wine exploration.

White
VOUVRAY
Made in the French Loire Valley from the Chenin Blanc grape, Vouvray's high acidity stands up to flavored hearty sauces and it typically has flavors of ginger, fig and nuts. It has the potential to age well and can be found in a few different styles—dry, off-dry and sweet. Try an off-dry Vouvray with a spicy masala full

of rich flavors, or a sweet Vouvray with my tarte tatin (*see* page 174).

VIOGNIER

This is the name of the grape variety known to produce naturally aromatic wines. Its fruit-driven style means it pairs well with spiced foods, especially the Californian and Australian wines that have hazelnut and stone fruit characteristics. Try with a mild, creamy fish recipe.

GEWÜRZTRAMINER

This wine has a natural sweetness and the scent and flavor of lychees: "gewürz" means spicy in German. You can now find good examples of this wine in other parts of the world. Try with spiced, nutty, fruity recipes such as my roast eggplant salad (*see* page 82).

RIESLING

This is a grape that originated in Germany but is now grown all over the world. Where it is grown will influence its taste, but typically it has a good balance of sugar and acidity that means it can handle the flavors from spicy dishes. Try a slightly sweet-tasting German Riesling with a hearty masala with a good level of chile.

Red

BEAUJOLAIS

Beaujolais is a wine region that uses the Gamay grape. A light-bodied, low-tannic wine with low to medium acidity, it works wonders with Indian dishes and can taste even better when slightly chilled. It typically has flavors of red berries and has been described as "the only white wine that happens to be red." Try with a creamy tomato-based dish with medium chile levels such as my Chicken Tikka Masala (*see* page 52).

CARMÉNÈRE

Originally grown in France, but now more so in Chile, this crimson wine has flavors of cherries and spice with some earthy undertones that make it great with Indian food. Try with my Slow-Roast Spiced Lamb (*see* page 44).

SYRAH (SHIRAZ)

This wine has always been a popular choice for its powerful flavors and fuller body. I often find it too heavy and prefer it when it has been blended and so becomes lighter in style and more palatable with heavily flavored meat dishes. Try with a spicy robust dish such as my Chile Beef with Black Pepper (*see* page 60).

Index

Biography

Anjali Pathak is an exciting talent in the Indian food and spice arena with a fun-loving and warm character. Having learned the basics of Indian cookery from a young age, Anjali has stepped out of her heritage and works with spice and flavors from across the globe. Not only is she the next generation of a family that brought Indian cuisine to households around the world, Patak's, she has an award-winning cookbook under her name and regularly appears at food festivals.

Anjali is a respected chef, food writer and cookery teacher and has been short-listed for a number of awards for her work with Indian food and flavors. With qualifications from the prestigious Leiths School of Food and Wine, Wine and Spirit Education Trust (WSET) and a diploma in Diet and Nutrition, Anjali continues to go from strength to strength, regularly appearing on television across the world. Anjali's work has appeared in leading international food and lifestyle media and her cookery master classes are always sold out.

Connect with Anjali online at www.anjalipathak.com or via Twitter and Instagram @anjali_pathak.

Acknowledgments

There are too many people I would like to thank who have helped bring my book to life. I won't ramble on but I need to thank my design team at Smith & Gilmour who have put my pages together with beauty and vibrance: you were a joy to work with and it looks better than I ever imagined. Thanks to my food stylist Aya and my photographer Martin, who not only shot the most beautiful images but who both had some great recipe ideas they were very keen to share! Eleanor, Polly and all the team at Octopus for persevering with me and meticulously going through my manuscript to make sure the book is perfect. I can't begin to tell you how pleased I am with it. To all my wonderful tasters, thank you all for lending me your taste buds.

A very special thank you to my wonderful agent Anne Kibel, who has supported all my wishes and continues to help my food dreams come true.

And finally, a very special thank you to my wonderful family and partner. No matter how crazy my dreams are, you are always by my side and your guidance is something I will never take for granted. You continue to inspire me to set my goals high, and with hard work I hope to make you proud. I wouldn't be who I am today if it weren't for you, so thank you for all you have done for me. I love you with all my heart.

Published in the United States by Clarkson Potter/Publishers,
an imprint of the Crown Publishing Group, a division of
Penguin Random House LLC, New York.
www.crownpublishing.com
www.clarksonpotter.com

CLARKSON POTTER is a trademark and POTTER with
colophon is a registered trademark of Penguin Random
House LLC.

Originally published in the United Kingdom by Mitchell
Beazley, a division of Octopus Publishing Group Ltd, London,
in 2015.

Library of Congress Cataloging-in-Publication Data
Pathak, Anjali.
    [Secrets from my Indian family kitchen]
    The Indian family kitchen / Anjali Pathak.
        pages cm
    Originally published: United Kingdom : Mitchell Beazley, a
division of Octopus Publishing Group Ltd, London, 2015.
under the title Secrets from my Indian family kitchen.
1. Cooking, Indian.   I. Title.
    TX724.5.I4P3485 2016
    641.5954--dc23

                        2015009566

ISBN 978-0-8041-8826-5
eBook ISBN 978-0-8041-8827-2

Printed in China

Design and art direction by Smith & Gilmour
Jacket design by Michael Nagin
Photography by Martin Poole

10 9 8 7 6 5 4 3 2 1

First Edition